SPIRIT COMMUNICATIONS

SPIRIT COMMUNICATIONS

Bob Woodward

ATHENA PRESS
LONDON

SPIRIT COMMUNICATIONS
Copyright © Bob Woodward 2007

All Rights Reserved

No part of this book may be reproduced in any form
by photocopying or by any electronic or mechanical means,
including information storage or retrieval systems,
without permission in writing from both the copyright
owner and the publisher of this book.

ISBN 10-digit: 1 84401 959 4
ISBN 13-digit: 978 1 84401 959 5

First Published 2007 by
ATHENA PRESS
Queen's House, 2 Holly Road
Twickenham TW1 4EG
United Kingdom

Printed for Athena Press

I dedicate this book in love to my niece's son, Mathew Clutton, who passed into Spirit on the eve of Ascension Day 2006, aged eleven years. He fought a long, hard, battle with bone marrow cancer and was, and is, a brave, courageous and loving soul.

Acknowledgments

I wish to express my sincere gratitude to all my guides and helpers in Spirit both known and, perhaps, so far, unknown, particularly, of course, to Joshua Isaiah and Dr John and to my dear mother and father.

Among all those 'in the body' who have taken an active interest and given positive support in the coming about of this book, I wish to mention especially my good friends, Anne, Cynthia and Per.

Once again, my thanks to Hazel, who, as with my other books, has miraculously transformed my handwritten script into readable type, and, of course, to my publishers who have dared to take this book on board!

But the time approaches, indeed it is already here, when those who are real worshippers will worship the Father in spirit and in truth. Such are the worshippers whom the Father wants. God is spirit, and those who worship him must worship in spirit and in truth.

> Jesus speaking to the woman of Samaria
> John 4:23–25

Foreword

> The gathering of such reports [self-reported external and internal psychic experiences of the populace] is useful for several reasons: one, for furthering the mappings of our understandings of the astonishing and seeming unending abilities that exist within 'normal' human nature; second, to give assurance to those who are 'sensitive' to these kinds of experiences, that events such as theirs have been similarly experienced by many throughout history; and third, to expand understanding that such are not the stuff of madness, but of an expanded and meaningful consciousness ... forms and expressions beyond ordinary reality that can augment our understandings of humanness.
>
> Clarissa Pinkola Estes, PhD

It is the conventional practice for the writer of a foreword to a work of this kind to possess some expertise in the author's subject. In this case, I cannot pretend to possess the skills in mediumship and spiritual healing that Bob describes, but can personally attest to his abilities in both these fields. My own background has no relevance, save that personal experience of a bewildering and often frightening kind as both a child and an adult has led me to believe unquestioningly in the existence of life after death. I had also experienced the benign 'miracle' of spiritual healing at a time of great distress in my personal life, which had reaffirmed for me my belief that human existence was meaningful and not just a glimpse of light between the darkness of the womb and the tomb, to paraphrase the writer Samuel Beckett.

I first met Bob when I came to him for a healing, following a chance meeting with X, a former client, who had told me, with great joy, about her new job as a cook in a Steiner school. This young woman had suffered from severe depression, exacerbated by the physical manifestation of the illness on her body. X suffered from eczema on her arms and hands – a painful and unsightly skin condition that had forced her to retire from cooking as a profession. She gleefully told me that she had met someone where she was currently working who had cured her eczema and, although it might come back again if she allowed herself to become too stressed, she was confident that he would be able to help her again. I was intrigued and arranged a meeting with this 'wonderful man'.

I had several agendas in mind when I made my initial phone call to Bob. I wanted first of all to make contact with this individual who had facilitated such a turnaround in the life of X, and to see if I felt sufficient trust in him to request healing for both myself and the clients on my caseload whose problems required more than just a 'talking treatment' to encourage them back to health. I also wanted to see if he would agree to present himself and his work to the sceptical questioning of the community mental health team in which I worked. Having great faith in the power of complementary therapies, and an enormous respect for the power of the mind to either overcome or create illness, I had been overjoyed when both a reflexologist and a homeopath joined our otherwise very medically orientated team. I was saddened, however, when they both chose to leave after a few years. I believe they felt that battering their heads against the very hard brick wall of the conventional 'medical model' was too damaging to their own mental health to be sustained for any length of time. I did feel, however, that their presence within the team had awakened an interest in alternative approaches to healing, and hoped that Bob's talk might provoke their curiosity and stimulate an appetite for further debate.

My initial visit to Bob, which included a healing, lifted both the headache with which I had arrived and my spirits. He kindly agreed to see me again and I forgot about my other agendas and just looked forward to my visits; to sitting in his small calm room surrounded by crystals and books, a universe away from the stressful environment of my own workplace. As our relationship grew in trust, Bob began to tell me about his relationship with the world of Spirit, and the communications he received from Joshua and Dr John, the two principal excarnate beings with whom he had established connection. As Bob read the communications he had received from his guide, Joshua, I realised that these were lessons for both of us. Like Bob, I needed to learn to trust in the wisdom of the heart as well as the head. I also learned the hard but necessary lesson that I had to take responsibility for the suffering I had experienced in this life, and to realise that I needed to let go of the anger that lay behind my drive to help other suffering human beings. Letting go of anger would fill my heart with love. This is a lifetime's task, maybe – vital for me and for all sentient beings.

In conclusion, as Bob and I continued to meet for healing and conversation, I hoped that my belief in what he was doing would encourage this modest and reticent man to trust more in his abilities as a psychic and a healer. I won't say more, for as you read this book you will see that I was in good company!

Dr Cynthia Morgan, PhD

The Author

By profession Bob Woodward is a curative educator, having lived with and taught children with special educational needs for over thirty years. He lives with his wife, Silke, and his family in a Camphill Community setting in Thornbury, near Bristol.

For the past seven years, Bob has been actively engaged in spiritual healing, and he is a full healer member of the Bristol District Association of Healers, and also recently of the National Federation of Spiritual Healers (NFSH). His active interest in spiritual healing goes back more than twenty-five years.

He gives healing to some children with special needs, with parental consent, and to adults by private arrangements. Bob is at present registered as a part-time PhD student with the Faculty of Health and Social Care at the University of the West of England, investigating how some children with special needs respond to receiving spiritual healing. He has two Masters' degrees from the University of Bristol, is the co-author of the book, *Autism – A Holistic Approach* and is the sole author of *Spirit Healing*, published by Floris Books in 2000 and 2004 respectively.

He has been a student of Rudolf Steiner's (1861–1925) anthroposophy, or spiritual science, for the past forty years, and is a member of the Anthroposophical Society in Great Britain.

Bob has many interests and his hobbies include walking and jogging in the countryside, reading, collecting crystals and most recently, in his sixtieth year, learning judo! He enjoys holidaying with his family, and sometimes alone, on the beautiful Isles of Scilly in Cornwall.

Contents

Introduction	17
Readings from a Medium	21
A Doubting Thomas	45
Communicating with Dr John	60
Communicating with Joshua (I)	74
Communicating with Joshua (II)	93
Communicating with Joshua (III)	110
Life in Spirit	125
Family Contacts and Requests	144
Review and Looking Forward	155
Conclusion	161
Suggested Reading	163
Postscript	165

Introduction

Why have I written this book and why at this particular time? The answers, quite simply, are these:

I feel I should share with others, as best I can, some of the communications that I believe I have been able to have telepathically with individuals who are no longer physically with us and thereby to help give positive reassurance that both life and consciousness do indeed continue beyond death. With regard to the timing, I feel that there is now a pressing need for many human beings on both sides of life to know of, and perhaps themselves find ways to engage in, such fruitful contacts and communications. So to speak, 'the time has come' to bridge the seemingly great divide that separates us from our loved ones and also from our guides and helpers in Spirit. As Rudolf Steiner predicted in the first quarter of the twentieth century, there should increasingly come about a conscious and cooperative communication and working together between the living and the so-called dead.

To engage in 'communication' is to enter into a mutual activity that is much more than being the mere recipient of one-way messages from the other side. It is rather an active and reciprocal process in which questions can be raised and answers given. There are, of course, a variety of means and ways in which communications may ordinarily take place between people. They can include, for example, verbal, visual, tactile, written or electronic forms and can be more or less direct, or distant, immediate or delayed in time. However, the form of communication described in this book is telepathic in nature as it consists of a direct, inner conversation in clear and articulate thoughts, which can, at the time it takes place, also be written down and recorded. The book will describe how these telepathic communications have come about over time, through taking up the opportunity that was offered to me by certain friends in Spirit. This was not something that I had previously seriously entertained or even necessarily wished for! I would even go so far as to say that for many years I have deliberately avoided attempts to have any personal contact with those who have died.

And yet there is no denying that it is one of the most pressing questions that quite ordinary people ask: is there any way in which we can know for sure, beyond simple belief or faith, that there is a life and existence after death? This question immediately loses all intellectual abstraction and purely philosophical speculation when, for example, a loved one dies in a family. On the contrary, it can then be felt to be a burning and existential issue for those who are left behind to pick up the pieces and, somehow, get on with their lives without the family member who is no longer – physically – there.

The feelings of profound loss and of grieving may perhaps be further compounded by deep feelings of guilt and remorse for what was done, or even left undone, when the now departed one was still there. But is death really the end of life and consciousness, or rather 'the birth' into a new and perhaps fuller life in Spirit, as many religions and faiths strongly assert? Above all, is there a way, or ways, in which genuine communication can be continued between those living in the material body and those who, through death, are now body-free? This brings us back to my reason for daring to write this book at this time, namely, to share at least one way in which such communications can take place. In doing so, I hope that what is written here may, in some measure, give others much needed reassurance and comfort and perhaps also encouragement to find their own way of having personal experiences that can confirm that the spirit world is not 'miles away' but actually here and now. As my medium friend once expressed it, 'the dead are but a thought away.'

Unlike my previous writings, this book contains no supporting references to other related literature, and there is no bibliography or index, (although I have added some suggested reading material at the end). This is because it is a sharing with the reader of my personal experiences and my pathway, or journey, in becoming aware of certain realities. Until now I have only shared a very small number of these communications with a few friends and family members. Moreover, I want to leave my readers quite free to come to their own conclusions and judgements about what is here offered. I am not setting out to convince or to argue a case by referring to other published sources. Each person must, of course, make up his or her own mind or, perhaps even more importantly, keep an open mind to possibilities rather than prematurely closing the doors tight shut. This open-mindedness is, I feel, also an important part of my own learning process.

I wish you light and love on your own personal quest for truth and knowledge of the Spirit.

Bob Woodward

April 2006, in Holy Week towards Easter

Readings from a Medium

For the past seven years I have been a healer. In actual fact my active interest in spiritual healing goes back for at least twenty-five years; but my direct practice of hands-on spiritual healing began when, very fortunately, I came into contact with Dennis and Doreen Fare at their healing centre in Kingswood, Bristol. I began my practical training with them in January 1999.

Over these past seven years I have again and again sought confirmation of my healing abilities, that is to say, of my abilities to serve as a channel for healing energies from others. Most recently, some fifteen months ago, I sought for this confirmation from a lady who had advertised her willingness to give individual postal readings, describing herself as a 'spiritual medium'. It was this 'spiritual' aspect that caught my eye in particular. I therefore wrote to Anne at her home in Yorkshire in late December 2004, enclosing as requested a passport-sized photograph of myself and a letter with several questions. The reply I received early in the New Year was the first of what then turned into a series of readings as I struck up a regular correspondence with my medium friend. Through these questions and answers, put to and received from Spirit, I became aware of two principal guides and helpers in my life: my spirit doctor and my spirit teacher. What now follows in this chapter is a selection of the contents from these readings, beginning with the first, dated 6 January 2005.

First Reading

> As I tune into your photograph and tune into your letter I see a spirit doctor stood behind you in a three-

quarter length white coat and dark trousers, and he has a round face. I cannot see his hair very clearly so I cannot determine if he hasn't got a lot of hair or I am unable to see it. He is directly behind you and he wishes to work with you in spiritual healing. He has worked with you for a while but he is telling me the link is a little tentative and that somehow your mind and thought processes on how the healing should work are actually preventing him from blending fully with you so that 100% of the healing that is required to be given can actually flow through you. I am given the feeling this slight imbalance, for want of a better word, is due to an interest you have in energies. As if you need to know exactly what energies are needed for you to be the channel for the healing? The doctor wishes you to know that the energies he channels through you are spiritual healing and, as such, it will be him that controls the healing energies; the amount and the formula they are made from. You are only the hosepipe or teapot through which the healing energies will travel.

So I feel with your question, 'What is needed to develop further my healing potential and abilities?' you have to decide which form of healing you wish to channel. Whether it is to channel healing energies you feel the patient needs as in reiki healing, where your energies and earth energies are used, or whether you want to be a channel for spiritual healing where you are not in control of those energies and you do not necessarily need to know the condition the patient is suffering from for healing to work. You need to trust the doctor behind you. I am being given the feeling that if you choose to use energies for e.g. reiki or other forms of healing that are not totally spiritual healing, the doctor will step back from doing the healing with you and someone who is more adept at the form of healing you choose will come forward.

The answer to the question, 'What is needed for my own self-healing?' is simple meditation. Listen to your heart and retreat into the silence; ask for Spirit to give you healing. Meditation develops the gifts of Spirit and it is also food for the soul, whereas meat and vegetables are food for the body. Regularly sitting in the silence, even if only for ten minutes, will allow the peace and healing to surround you and, if you listen, you will receive strength, guidance and understanding of what the true form of healing is.

In this first reading from Anne others came through to me from Spirit and then the reading was concluded with the following words:

They say the reading is coming to an end and that you are a light worker and what a joy you are to be with and to blend with you when you work. They give their love and respect and wish that the answers to your questions have not caused offence or any confusion in your pathway. They say sit and feel the answers you have been given and see if just like a Christmas jumper it fits, or if it doesn't put it away until you think it might and try it on again.

The doctor in Spirit says he will continue to work with you in the best way he can whilst you contemplate your future pathway in the healing fraternity.

They wish you peace and love until you walk into their arms on the other side, then all will be made clear and you will see the great distance you have travelled.

On the basis of this reading and with regard to my practice of healing, I made further efforts in my inner attitude of trust towards my role as healer as a channel and transmitter of the energies directed from Spirit. I wanted to confirm that spiritual healing was my chosen form of healing and that I did indeed wish to work cooperatively with my spirit-doctor.

After several weeks I wrote again to Anne with further questions, and received a reply from her dated 10 February 2005.

Second Reading

When I ask the question; 'Is the spirit doctor working with you doing spiritual healing finding it easier to blend with you during healing sessions?' I get the feeling as I look at your photograph that he is stood behind you and he tells me there is a clearer line of communication opened. There has been a reduction in your thoughts as you do healing so that he is able to come closer to you. Your aura has become calmer and there is less disruption around you from unwanted thoughts.

He is telling me it is continued relaxation of thoughts that has helped and will continue to help you in the future. He is encouraging you to sit in the silence and, rather than mental concentration, he is advocating a relaxed mind, so that if thoughts come into it you do not concentrate on getting rid of them but continue with in and out breathing and ignore the thoughts. That way your mind will be more receptive to spirit communication because your attention is relaxed.

The doctor is giving me the feeling he is very pleased with how much progress has been made and he says you are a good pupil of good intent and dedication to help others. Again he is wearing his white coat but I do not see his features clearly. I get the feeling this doctor was used to strict discipline and that he continues to like order in how he can work.

Another question that I had written to Anne was to do with the perhaps somewhat unusual reaction, or response, I experienced when holding quartz crystals. After a short time my hands would begin to vibrate, quite vigorously, when I held such crystals. The spirit doctor gave an answer to this question and also spoke of other interesting aspects of the effects of crystals, but it would go too far to elaborate fully on this here. Suffice it to quote that having mentioned the possibility of my having an 'intentional tremor', that is where, for example, the cup and saucer rattles when you try to hold them, he said:

> 'The other more likely reason is that you are very sensitive to the vibrations of the crystals. Many people feel the vibrations of the crystals as either heat or cold or tingling. If you are sensitive to them it could make your arms vibrate or twitch. If you wanted to overcome this, it would be possible to desensitise yourself to the vibrations by working with the crystals on a regular basis.'

I had also asked Anne whether my parents, both deceased, had anything they wished to say to me.

> Your parents are giving me a contented feeling that they know you accept they are well in Spirit and leading their own lives. They will eventually, when it is your time, be there to meet you when you go over to Spirit. I get the feeling they may not make their presence known to you very often and this is because they feel there is not a need to do so. They are only a thought away, and I feel you often talk to them in your thoughts and they say they respond with thoughts to you and they say how lucky they are to be able to maintain that link.

I have included these more personal family communications as they may help bring comfort and reassurance to those who read them that our loved ones are never very far away even when they are no longer to be seen with ordinary eyes. Indeed, they are 'only a thought away'.

Having received communications from my spirit doctor through Anne the medium in the first two readings, I felt that I now wanted to know more about him. What was his name; his background; how long had he been working with me; did he also help when I asked for absent healing (healing at a distance) for people? I received Anne's reply a month later on 10 March 2005.

Third Reading

The doctor answered:

> 'For the purposes of this enquiry my name is Dr John Cahill.' ['I am not sure of the spelling,' wrote Anne.] 'I was born in Michigan in the USA. I was of peasant stock you would say and I was one of the first in my family to graduate with a doctorate. My life mainly dealt with psychiatry and its relevant social consequences. I was known in my field, but not widely known. When I passed I carried my interest forward with me and I spent time researching and learning about the mental attitudes and our upbringings that make us who we are, and how when we pass it affects our transition and how we perceive the afterlife to be. This has a great interest to me and is very relevant in helping people with their transition. Now I work through healers, one of them is you, to help manipulate the mental states and mental outlooks as well as other psychiatric encumbrances to see if we as spirit doctors can assist before the transition, so that it will enable an easier recovery into Spirit whereby all faculties are restored.

'I wish to reassure you that I am also a general doctor and can perform healing as instructed by my higher guides on a variety of conditions. As you may be aware, as a spirit doctor if we are not fully qualified in the field in which we are asked to perform healing, we will ask our colleagues who have that knowledge to perform that healing. This is why it is not advisable for a healer to become fixed on a doctor in Spirit to perform the healing, because that doctor may not be the most appropriate one to do the healing. By asking for the most appropriate person to channel the healing for the patient the healing will be the best that they can give.'

To the question, 'How long have you been working with me, and for how long could this continue?' the reply was:

'I have been around you in a concrete way for around five years. If you call on me to do the healing then I will make myself available to you for as long as it is possible to do so. If we continue to perform together in the way that we do, then I see no reason why our relationship should not continue for as long as there are people who need the healing energies that I can offer.'

When asked; 'Do you work with me when I request absent healing for people as well as when I give direct, hands-on, spiritual healing?' the reply was:

'Yes, I am the one who receives your requests and, if the person is within my area of working, then if it is appropriate for me to do the healing I will do so. If the person is a long distance away from a condition I know, my colleagues can work better and have a more advanced knowledge and I will pass the request on to them. The most appropriate person will then be assigned to carry out the healing with that patient. The healing will also continue in their sleeping state for as long as it is requested or required.'

The last question I had put, to do with healing *per se*, was this one: 'I believe that unconditional love is the most important, or the essence, of the healing energies and that this comes from the Christ Spirit in response to our requests for healing. Is this correct?'

'Yes, that is correct. In practical terms there is spiritual healing energy that helps in the spiritual side and there is also, depending on the condition, a mixture of solar, gamma and other rays. This is a spiritual science. The healing energies are prescribed, mixed, and channelled from Spirit. Although as you will see, as everything is held together with love, the universe is held together and motivated by love, then it is true that the healing energies come from the Godhead, the Christ Spirit, but are manipulated in ways that can affect the physical body and this is helped by the channelling through a human into a human. Although remember we are spirit in a physical body not a body with a spirit.'

Being a student of the writings and work of the Austrian philosopher, educator, and spiritual-scientist, Rudolf Steiner (1861–1925), for some forty years I had also asked this question for this third reading. 'Do you know the works of Rudolf Steiner?' The reply was:

'Yes, he was a man of a wide vision, of knowledge of the essence of who we are. To some extent I did read and know of his works although when one comes to Spirit one does not follow a particular person's way of thinking. One develops a more spiritual way of thinking and this spiritual doctorship is the way forward that I have taken. I now work under the guidance of the healing master in the academy of medicine in Spirit.'

In conclusion Dr John added the following:

'I hope I have answered your questions to a satisfactory degree and I wonder whether you would feel, as I feel, that if we could meet in the silence where you could begin to feel my presence, that this would be a more satisfactory way of communication than meeting through a medium, albeit a medium who also is walking under the guidance of the healing master.

'I am more than willing to come to you when you ask to sit in the silence so that we can begin, or should I say continue our relationship, because by blending together in the silence it helps when we do our healing work. The blending is more companionable and there are less restrictions of the healing energy. So I wish you well, my friend, until we meet again, God bless you.

Anne added the comment:

It was lovely to meet your doctor, although I did not see him today. He spoke very clearly and I have transcribed his words as best I can.

So in this third reading a definite opportunity, and a challenge, was put towards me, namely, to no longer rely on my medium friend to enter into communication with my spirit doctor – whom I refer to as Dr John – but to link up with him directly when sitting in the silence.

Over the following months I continued nonetheless to put my various questions via Anne and each time waited patiently for the readings to arrive through the post. The reader must understand that it is only possible for me to select from these readings certain parts which clearly show the process that was unfolding in my growing awareness of my work with Dr John and his colleagues, and also my introduction to my guide and teacher in Spirit who, for the first time, clearly came through to Anne in the fourth reading, dated 15 April 2005.

Fourth Reading

The reading from Anne began with impressions from my parents, and then moved on to Dr John.

> I now see a white coat and your doctor makes his presence felt. I ask him your first question about being a healer in another incarnation, his reply is: 'It is not for me to answer that, it is for your guides to give you that direction.'

My second question to him was about the importance or not of the healer giving a description of a patient's ill condition when requesting healing help. Dr John's reply was:

> 'It is always appropriate where possible to give a general description of the impediments and anxieties of the particular patient. This is so that we can have a general indication of which direction the healing will be given, so that at the beginning of the healing regime we can allocate the appropriate healing people to that person. If we have a request for healing and no direction of the problem, then it just means we have to spend further time around the person to actually examine and find out what the problem is. But quite often the problem that presents itself is not necessarily

what the patient is complaining about; it is often the small things that result from the illness such as stress, emotional trauma, that if we are given the direction to look in that area we can activate the help just a little quicker.

'If I can give an example to you: if a person is diabetic and asks for help then we will send down the appropriate person to give healing around the pancreas, liver, and work out the blood sugar levels, but if the healer is aware that the main complaint of the person is night leg cramps caused by reduced circulation because of the diabetes, then we can immediately give the appropriate healing to help with the leg cramps during the night. Whereas if we were not told of this problem it might take another night before we were to see the extent of the problem for the patient. In the long term it does not matter if we have notification of the exact problem but, in the short term, it is of help in making the easement of conditions quicker. Do not feel a lack of knowledge of medical conditions on your part makes the healing you channel less efficient. It is enough for you to visualise the person and ask for the most appropriate person to give the healing.'

To another question about my healing work with some children with special needs, Anne wrote:

The doctor says you know it is a good thing to do and it is good for them. He says their souls are contained within a body that is not functioning to the optimum, but they still respond to love and need the care and attention that you can give them. Your healing is of immense importance to these children not only for now but with their connection between the physical and the spiritual, because they can feel frustration and anger within their own bodies. With the help of Spirit it can enhance the feelings and emotions that need enhancing and also quieten the more unnerving thoughts and feelings they have. Physically the healing also helps but they cannot show you the great benefit they get from it.

I also had a question about making times for me to come into direct contact with Dr John and also what sort of communication this would be.

He says that, as you are a mentally active person, he will be able to access this area for communication and you will be able to hear his voice in your head. Do not be impatient with this because his thoughts will be in your voice not his. You will have to be aware of your thoughts to determine which are his words and which are yours. To help you do this, when you sit in the quiet he will give you a gentle peacefulness in the room where you sit. You will know when you recognise this he will be about and will respond to your questions by thought...

He himself is a more mentally orientated person and as such your communications will be mainly by clairaudience. This is the most accurate way of communication he says and for you to keep trying until you are confident that it is not all in your head.

He says the healing is working and you are a team and if you wish to continue with it he will remain with you. He would be very happy if you could put aside fifteen minutes two to three times a week so that your working relationship could be strengthened and your guides could come close and give you the teachings you want to know, because your guides have been picked especially to be able to communicate with you and understand your pathway and outlook on life, so they are the better qualified people to give you the advice and teachings you seek.

As Anne was doing the reading, she commented just at this point:

> As I am saying this I am being shown a Jewish cap – it is one of your guides who is acknowledging what I have just said. He is a Jewish elder and he is now showing me a ceremonial either apron or sash that he would wear in the synagogue as part of his uniform. It is white or cream in colour and has tassels on the end. I cannot see it clearly and do not have the knowledge of what he is trying to show me. I hope you can understand what I am describing. It would go round his waist or neck. He is encouraging you to make your sitting time a regular thing so that spirits know when they can come and teach you.

So with this I was given an introduction, so to speak, to at least one of my main guides, or teachers, on the other side of life. Anne concluded her reading to me by writing: 'With love and the confidence that you are on the right path.'

Once again the possibilities and opportunities for me to come into direct, mental communication and contact with Dr John and with Spirit, had been clearly expressed. As the reader will no doubt easily imagine, I had numerous questions and, once again, turned to Anne, to provide me with some answers!

Fifth Reading

In a short reading, dated 13 May 2005, Anne wrote:

> As I sat and asked your doctor to come close to answer your questions, it was the learned gentleman who answered – the Jewish elder. He said that whilst Dr John was around you for the healing there were other guides who were with you more often. One of them is

himself and he is there to answer your questions and queries on spirit matters and philosophy.

He tells me that yes the people around you will come through to you the same way as Dr John and you just need to be open-minded enough to start up a relationship with them. To listen in the same way and get a feel of their different communications, because each of your guides has a different personality and if you ask them to make contact in different ways, so that you can differentiate between them, they will do so.

Firstly, if you would like a physical feeling, then ask them to give their sign to you – each will be different. Then if you wish for a mental sign, this way you build up a confidence of who each of them are. Just as you have taken time with John, spend time with your other friends and remember that when you work closely with Spirit they will bring in from time to time 'spirit friends' who will have been invited by your guides to give you a teaching one way or the other, either through conversation or demonstration. Do not assume that every spirit who comes to talk is a guide, just take them for what they are: beings of light that wish to come and communicate with you. If you sit in the love and the light with your guides there will be no disruptive spirit communication. They give this to reassure you rather than put you off communication, because I know you are a sensitive and sensible person and will develop an understanding of Spirit on all the levels that are shown to you.

I wish you good sitting and listening!

Well, no doubt I had experimented by May/June 2005 with trying to sit in the silence and becoming receptive to communications from Dr John in the first place. However, I cannot now remember any of the details of these early attempts to distinguish thoughts received from friends across the threshold from my own thoughts. I did not record these earlier attempts at linking up consciously and the entries in my first notebook, when I did begin to commit these communications to paper, only start in July 2005. However, it is clear from the contents of the sixth reading, which I received from Anne on 17 June 2005, that I had indeed been trying to sit and listen.

Sixth Reading

Anne writes:

> As I sit to read your letter, I am aware of a gentleman in Spirit who has come to be the communicator. He says you are well known to Spirit for you are a regular worker for the light:
>
> 'It is always easy to call on one's friends when the links of communication have been made. Bob knows the answers to his questions; he just needs confirmation from you. If you give information that does not quite match his information, whom is Bob going to believe then? We know that Bob should believe his own heart and any misunderstandings he has would only be minor ones because the communication link has been made. Yes his doctor is able to speak to him and guide his work, but I am the gentleman who has the Jewish connection he wishes to communicate with. This I have done, but he is a little uncertain, so I will speak to him through you if that is acceptable to you, my dear friend.
>
> 'Bob is still asking for physical confirmation rather than listening to the guidance he has received. That is understandable at this stage of development, but I ask that he does indeed trust. If he can trust us, why does he not trust himself for he is one of us, and if we did not trust him we would not be around to ask him to do our work.'

Owing to various outer circumstances around this time, it had not been possible for me to continue with my healing work with the children, and this is referred to in what follows in the reading.

'Because the physical things around you change, it does not mean that things are going wrong or not according to plan. The physical world spins and turns, but we must stay steadfast to our connection to the divine. If the physical opportunities change, then we adapt the lessons accordingly. So if there is a pause in the healing then it is not detrimental because healing will continue from Spirit as best as we can do, but it gives us an opportunity to continue or start a lesson on a different subject. Although I was Jewish, and that is how I show myself, that is purely for confirmation and recognition. I have gone beyond the bounds of religion and it is as a spirit with a true heart that I come to work with you, Bob.

'I beseech you to take the time out and sit so that we can do learning exercises together. You may feel the sitting is an inconvenience, but if you do not attend school you will not learn the lessons prepared for you. I have been asked to open doorways of knowledge and understanding for you and it is for this reason, and this reason only, that I ask that you send your thoughts to me and continue to arrange a sitting on a regular basis. If you can do it once a week, Bob, then do that; if you can do it twice a week there will be double the benefit.

'The information and the guidance you are getting will not be earth-shattering, but they do come from the divine and they will allow you to use your gifts to the benefit of mankind. Yes we know where your heart strives in the healing of the dear children and we know you will have a great battle with those purely of the physical who do not recognise the true being of who we are. I have taken this opportunity to speak to you personally, though I do speak to you in your quiet moments. You are beginning to recognise the tone of my words...

'Bob, give heart you no longer need to utilise this medium, although I know she is more than willing to participate in your future development. I will now allow her to read your letter and receive the appropriate answers to the questions that you ask.

'My name is Joshua Isaiah M—'

[Anne commented here: 'Sorry, Bob, I could not pronounce his surname and when he flashed in front of me I only saw the M, a few letters down there was a J and I think an F, it was not clear as it was so fast.']

'I will give him more information on myself personally; he will accept it and not question your answer, so I ask Bob that you strive to get the answers from me. I will tell you my name, where I was brought up, how I died and why I feel a connection to you. That is part of building up the relationship between us.'

One of the questions I had asked was whether a portrait in my room, done by a psychic artist, was a likeness of him (Joshua Isaiah). He replied through Anne:

'Of the portrait you feel is a drawing of me. If you sit and look at it I will look through your eyes and see the vibration. I will let you know how good a representation it is of me ... Any picture will be as a poor reflection in a mirror.'

Joshua then answered a question I had with regard to my healing work, and then added:

'I ask that you still sit to learn the knowledge with me as I can put opportunities for development before you. There is no need to answer the fourth question as to whether your friends in Spirit have anything they wish to say to you because that is what I am doing at this moment. I will be with you the evening you receive this letter and I ask that you sit and we will begin the lessons more intensely.

'Shalom, my friend. I am always around you and God bless you, my friend, for participating in this message. Shalom to you both.'

Anne added:

As this gentleman withdraws, I see an open book with a bookmark being placed in it. It is a religious book and the bookmark cream or white cloth with gold embroidery on it. The book is gently closed to finish the lesson. Bob, your friend came quite close to me for this letter and I gave as true a message as I could for you.

Up to this point I had been asking for, and receiving from Anne, readings on a more or less monthly basis, i.e. over the period from January to June 2005. Three months elapsed between the sixth and the seventh reading, which was dated 15 September 2005. Both Dr John and Joshua had things to tell me in answer to my questions.

Seventh Reading

When I ask your first question, 'Is Dr John pleased with the way the healing work is going, does he have any requests to make to you?' the answer I get is that he is pleased with the result. You have seen some good results with the healing; therefore do not question whether the healing is going all right or not, just trust that the healing as appropriate is being given and that healing efficiency cannot always be measured by recordable outcomes. There are infinite ways in which the healing energies permeate the body to produce an acceleration of healing time and also to work with the minute molecules that help in the emotional aspect of life. So trust that through your connection to Spirit the appropriate healing will be given.

There will be times when Dr John will call upon other healing friends in Spirit to help with the conditions that present themselves to you. He has the expertise of bones but there are certain areas that his companions in Spirit are more adept at dealing with. At these times they will come forward either to channel the healing through you or to work alongside Dr John whilst he works through you. As you become aware of the changing vibrations around you do not be perturbed if the comfortable vibrations of Dr John are slightly changed as other people make their presence felt.

My second question was about inwardly asking Dr John if the healing was going all right when I was actually giving someone hands-on healing.

He gives me the clairsentient feeling that it would be more appropriate to ask the questions when the healing has finished, when you are sat in your quiet time with him. It is not that your questions hamper the healing, it is just that your attention and his are being used to talk to each other whilst healing is going on and he gives me the feeling that in the quiet time he can give you a more detailed explanation of what has been happening. He also acknowledges that the conversations between you are helping to build up a working relationship and he quite enjoys intellectual discussions between you as you have some piercing questions that are not always easy to answer.

I had also asked Anne to put the question to my friends in Spirit if they felt I was making satisfactory progress as a healer and a medium (the latter referring to the reception of telepathic communications which I had been practising as suggested by them).

She wrote:

> The answer from Joshua is yes and these little tests or opportunities for development are being given to you as you have made progress with further progress to be made in the future. You do have the innate gift to develop into a competent medium giving philosophy through you. Your biggest challenge, as you are a thinker, will be to trust the words that are given to you and not assume they are your own thoughts.

The 'little tests or opportunities' referred to above were given, in the context of this particular reading, in the form of certain pictures which came to Anne to pass on to me. The intention was to give me the opportunity to practice my mediumship. For example, one such exercise was the possibility of getting into contact with Anne's deceased father and then to pass the information thus obtained back to her for feedback. I was left quite free as to whether I would attempt to do this or not. As it was, I did receive information which Anne later confirmed was largely consistent with her father's character: I had given, it seemed, quite a good reading.

Another question I had asked was whether Joshua would be happier if I was just receptive to him or if it was all right for me to ask questions.

Anne replied:

> He gives me the feeling that both are acceptable. If the question is urgent then ask him. He is aware of what

your questions are because of your thoughts, and he will try to answer your questions, when you sit in the silence, in a roundabout way in the form of teachings to allow you to answer the questions yourself. He says there is no rush to learn as all the answers are inside you and by sitting in the silence the answers will be allowed to reveal themselves.

After this there came to Anne a very mundane image!

I have now been shown a leg of meat from a butcher. It is raw and skinned. Clairsentiently I feel you may have been asking questions about meat as food. The next thing they show me is a white ring; it is similar to a polo mint or a support for the hole in filing paper that some people use, or even a circle of light.

When I ask why I have been given these things Joshua says they have been given for you to concentrate on in the silence and as you think of each one he will come close and give you some thoughts on them.

As the reading comes to a close he draws my attention to the bottom of your letter where it says, 'Trust is the keyword and a confirmation between friends.' He smiles as he gives you these exercises to do.

When I received this reading from Anne, I later sat in the silence and pictured the two images given by Joshua: 'the leg of raw meat' and 'the circle of light'. The interpretations given me were: the body of flesh – the being incarnated in dense matter – and the linking up with Spirit; the linking between the earthly world and the world of Spirit.

Another three months passed before I wrote, before Christmas, to Anne asking for another reading from her. I received her reply in the New Year, dated 3 January 2006.

Eighth Reading

The reading was four pages long, contained various pictures and images, and the communications from both Joshua and Dr John very much related to my/our healing work. However, interesting information was also given concerning different modes of communication as such.

> Joshua says that he is giving the information in symbols because, although you can hear his words, this is a way of practising other forms of communication; this is a way he will use to exercise your abilities. He will give you your own symbols and you will be able to feel if your interpretation is correct or not. Again we are talking levels of communication, he says; verbal communication he shows me is represented by the first third of a ruler and two-thirds are made up of pictures and feelings. He says he can communicate more utilising all three skills with you than just words. He now shows me his ringlets just to give evidence that it is he.
>
> He is pleased at the levels of communication you have between you, because not only is he smiling but he looks younger and more vibrant than he showed himself before. It is as if he also is flourishing with the work that you are both doing.
>
> Then I turn over the letter and you mention your communication to Joshua on a telepathic thought level and that works for you at the moment and you suspect thinkers are doubting Thomases, again Joshua smiles and says he is expanding your perspectives by giving you pictures and feelings. Again he says to balance your abilities for when situations arise, when you will need to use more than verbal input from Spirit. He also says to keep the balance to sitting in the silence equal to the periods of sitting with mental activity, because I am being shown scales and at the moment there is

more on the thinking level than on the silence side. He shows me that you can only get so much thinking in the head and then the silence is necessary to declutter the brain... This is the way he is trying to encourage you to work.

Just as an addition to this, when you say about strengthening your trust in Spirit he says trust comes from the heart. It has nothing to do with the mental level because that is more physical and can be manipulated by thought processes, whereas trust that comes from the heart, he gives me the words, 'Well of eternity, remains the same no matter which way it flows.'

After this certain details and new developments to do with the healing work with children, and involving more colleagues than Dr John, were communicated in the reading. Finally Anne concluded by writing:

When I read through your letter one last time and ask Spirit if there is anything else they wish to say, Joshua tells me he is around you every evening just before you drop off to sleep and you can talk to him and hear his answers in an informal way, as well as sitting at formally arranged times...

In love, light and truth always, Anne.

These eight readings had been spread over the course of one year, from January 2005 to January 2006. They had opened doors for me which I had neither imagined nor in any sense expected. Opportunities had been given to me which, whilst in no way imposed, also presented challenges.

I will conclude this first chapter by sharing some words received from another medium at the end of November 2005, to whom I had written to request a reading, but to whom I had as such posed no questions nor given any information about myself.

Spirit are saying, my friend, you have been through a struggle, spiritual and emotional (what do I believe, which way do I go).

You walk and feel the wind upon your face. My friend, you question many things and have doubts, you analyse and analyse; even these words from Spirit you will question. There is nothing wrong in this.

Stop, stand still. Spirit are trying to guide you. You have in your heart confusion, which blocks a deep knowledge, which we of the spirit world are trying to bring forward. We watch you as you walk, we are very aware of the darkness and pain which you have come through. This has left you somewhat sceptical and you must know the truth; this is good, for you must not accept blindly all that is said to you.

But believe we are with you, for you have much to give. Your courage is an inspiration; you are reluctant to speak to others of the deep spiritual wisdom which is yours, because you doubt it yourself; you are being guided.

And later:

Bob, the angel that has come forward for you is Gabriel. The keywords from Gabriel are: change, messages, spiritual growth, signs and guidance...

Sometimes change is frightening, because we are stuck in our old ways, but we need to welcome changes that bring us back to our true purpose.

To find our true purpose in life – is this not something which, in one way or another, each of us is seeking for?

A Doubting Thomas

As I remarked at the start of the last chapter, I have again and again over the past seven years sought for confirmation of my abilities as a healing channel from others. Considering the fact that I have also again and again had confirmation of the reality of the healing given through me, evidenced in the actual improvements of most of those who have come to me for healing, any additional confirmations sought might well be considered superfluous and unnecessary. That I have nonetheless done this says something, I feel, about the degrees of trust and faith and confidence in my own abilities and myself – or rather, at times at least, the lack of these!

It was out of this same feeling of wanting to receive confirmation primarily for my healing tasks that I turned in the first place to Anne, the spiritual medium, which in turn led to the sequence of eight readings from her. In the very first of these readings the first sentence was: 'As I tune into your photograph and tune into your letter I see a spirit doctor stood behind you ...' So, right from the word go, so to speak, I was given the concrete confirmation that I was looking for!

Looking back some years, I well remember another confirmation that was given to me after I had been involved in hands-on spiritual healing for about six months, training at that time with Mr and Mrs Fare, both healers with decades of experience.

I had arrived at Bill Harrison's Healing Weekend (which had become a very successful annual summer event), at Wedmore in Somerset. My intention was to help out in the

Bristol District Association of Healers tent as a probationer healer. That is to say, I thoroughly expected to be assisting either Dennis or Doreen in giving healing to any members of the public that wanted this. You can therefore imagine my surprise, even shock, when Doreen seriously suggested, and expected, that I could proceed with giving healing alone! Such was Doreen's confidence in me. Naturally both Dennis and Doreen would be well able to see what I was doing and perhaps even step in if need be, but still the thought of actually going it alone threw me into immediate confusion. What was I to do? Well, of course, I did what any self-negating doubting Thomas would do and headed out of the healing tent pronto, proceeding to wander around the various other tents and stalls set up in Bill's large back garden.

In one tent there were demonstrations of reiki healing, in another someone sat ready to read your palms when theirs was crossed with silver, and as I thus wandered about I wrestled inside myself with what I was going to do. I certainly felt I was not competent enough to return to the healing tent and give healing. After all, I reasoned, members of the public had the right to expect to be treated by experienced and qualified practitioners, which I was not. So, troubled by this dilemma, I entered the big marquee where a demonstration of mediumship and psychic painting was about to take place. I seated myself on a chair in the back rows and watched as people filled up the front rows; this seemed quite a good place to hide out for a while.

The medium, a lady, took the stage and proceeded to do whatever she did. To be honest, I had little interest in these things. However, she had also introduced the psychic artist, Patrick Gamble, and explained that while she did her mediumship, Patrick would be sitting at his easel and painting the spirit guide of someone in the audience; who that would be was a mystery for now. And so the show went on, so to speak, and sitting near the back I was certainly aware that, from time to time, Patrick Gamble, who was busily applying colours to his painting board, was looking over in my direction. I had the impression that something was up.

After perhaps half an hour it was clear that Patrick's painting was nearly completed. The medium asked that no one leave the marquee until it was established who the painting was for. The artist stood up, holding in his hands his finished work, and came down from the stage. He proceeded to walk around the audience until eventually he stopped in front of me and duly presented me with the painting, saying, 'This is for you.' I was surprised to be singled out in this way and yet I had had the distinct impression whilst Patrick was painting that my number was up, so to speak! The medium stepped down from the stage and escorted me up on the stage – so much for remaining incognito.

Patrick had the gift of seeing but not, it seems, of hearing Spirit. Therefore, it was left to the medium to tell me something about the person whose portrait was shown in the painting. The face was that of a brown-skinned Indian-looking man, with a rather anxious expression in his eyes, and wearing a large purple turban with a background of blue. She told me his name (which I soon forgot), that he was, or rather had been, a fisherman from Goa on the west coast of India, and that he was handing me a basket of fish as a gift. The medium asked me if I had anything to do with healing, to which I mumbled some reply, and then assured me that my Indian friend was saying I could do it!

So the answer to my inner dilemma was given in a way that I had certainly not foreseen when I left the healing tent three quarters of an hour before. I was pleased with what I had received so unexpectedly that morning, but also still trying to take in what had happened. I went out of the marquee, passed by the healing tent, left a message with someone that I needed to go, and headed for the car park. Near the exit, someone commented that the painting had lots of healing shown in it. I drove home and bought a wooden frame for the painting, which looks down on me from the top of my book shelves as I write these words. This was confirmation that I could be a healer and I am now also immediately reminded of how it was that I came into hands-on healing altogether.

I met Dennis and Doreen Fare for the first time in early October 1998, when I arrived at their house in Kingswood, Bristol, to keep an appointment to receive some healing for my right thumb. I had been given the address of The Dennis Fare Healing Centre by Mr Ray Branch of The Harry Edwards Spiritual Healing Sanctuary at Shere in Surrey. (In 1973 I had met Harry Edwards himself, briefly, at his country sanctuary.) For perhaps twenty years I had been in contact with the sanctuary to request absent healing for various people, including occasionally myself. My right thumb was a case in point as, having been broken in a school hockey game many years before, it could sometimes get quite achy and stiff in the joint. I thought that some direct contact healing might help and, for this reason, had the great good fortune to come into contact with the Fares. I was very interested and drawn to the spiritual healing work which they conducted in their own home on a Tuesday morning and a Thursday evening, and went to see them several more times in October and also in November and December that year.

On one occasion, I well remember Doreen telling me with conviction that she was sure that I could do healing myself if I wished to. She described how this certainty had come to her, possibly even through Harry Edwards himself. (He died in 1976.) Well I was definitely interested in the idea of training with and learning from Dennis and Doreen, but, at present, they had no vacancy for taking on any more trainees. With this in my mind, Christmas arrived and we looked ahead to the New Year, 1999. Suddenly, it seemed, the opportunity presented itself out of the blue. A young man who had been training with the Fares had had to pull out, for whatever reason, and so there was now a space for me to begin with them that January, if I so wished. On Thursday 7 January I arrived at their healing centre, donned a white coat (which was the custom at that time) and began my first year of practical hands-on training in healing. Without a shadow of a doubt, it was due to the confidence which Dennis and Doreen Fare invested in me, and their expert guidance, that I completed my first year as a trainee with them.

It would easily be possible to continue to describe my pathway into what Dr John, in one of Anne's readings, described as 'the healing fraternity'. However, this is not the main theme of this present book, which is concerned with spirit communication. Suffice it to say that, looking back, it is not very difficult to see how my way was guided – first by carrying on my training with a local healer when I was unable to continue with Dennis and Doreen, and later by working with a group of seven or eight healers who offered a weekly evening session for any members of the public. In spite of this, the doubting Thomas in me continued to seek for further confirmations that I was on the right path and, by now, I have not just the one original Indian portrait by the psychic artist Patrick Gamble in my study, but also three more portraits by him done in private sittings. Each is very different, but all attest to my healing abilities (or better said, my abilities to channel healing from Spirit). Indeed, the second portrait, which I received in April 2000 shows a bespectacled professional-looking man, whom Patrick described as holding a doctor's bag in which there were remedies for many types of illnesses! I hope that sharing something of my personal way into healing and an acknowledgement of the guidance which is working, so to speak, behind the scenes, may be helpful and even encouraging to those who also feel a calling in this direction in their lives.

When the Disciple Thomas (the twin) was not prepared to believe the words of the other disciples that the Risen Christ had appeared to them on the evening of Easter Sunday, he was, we could say, acting like any typical modern human being who has been brought up and lives in a scientific and sceptical world culture, where seeing is believing. Thomas needed to have the evidence of his own eyes, of his own senses, before he was prepared to accept that Christ's continued presence, after the death on Good Friday, was in fact a reality. This reality was, we are told, confirmed for Thomas personally one week later when, once again, Jesus came and stood among them and invited the doubting disciple to actually touch the places of his wounds:

> Reach your finger here; see my hands. Reach your hand here and put it into my side. Be unbelieving no longer, but believe.
>
> John 20:27

To my mind to follow in the footsteps of Thomas the doubter who then, through clear and indisputable personal evidence, became as much a believer of the Lord's reality as his fellow disciples is no bad thing. It is, I believe, preferable to being so completely trusting as to swallow everything one is told, 'hook, line and sinker', without a moment's reflection or thought, or without some sort of confirmation. It is no doubt a fine line to tread between trust and gullibility. We know often enough in everyday experience that many judgements we make about other people need to be adjusted in the light of further information or even prove to be completely false and incorrect!

In the present context then, what sort of 'touchstones' can one use in deciding for oneself upon the authenticity, plausibility, and credibility of information and insight which are given to you via a medium in the first place, and, in the second place, when the medium for such communications is oneself? I suggest that the touchstones needed will be precisely those that we use every day in our dealings and communications with other people that we meet, and perhaps particularly with complete strangers. Like Thomas, we need to be able to rely upon our healthy individual faculties of perceiving and thinking.

If, as I did, we request a reading from a medium, then we need to be clear about such essentials as:

- our own motivations and intentions;
- the sorts of questions we ask;
- the quality and tone, as well as the actual contents of the replies we receive; and
- what we do with this.

With regard to the tone and contents of the communications, it is, I believe, very important that we feel that our freedom, choices, and decisions are acknowledged and respected and not overruled. I think anyone receiving a message from another living person, or a person over the threshold, should be very wary of any hint of coercion, pressure, or demand, especially if in any way this would run counter to one's own ethics and code of conduct. There are unfortunately scoundrels, hoaxers, flatterers, and con men to be found aplenty on this side of life, and it is not to be assumed, I feel, that the act of leaving the body at death and entering into the other side will automatically confer morality, decency and considerateness on a person, if they have not been evident in his or her life before their passing!

It is certainly a great strength of human nature and human potential that people can, if they have the will to do so, change themselves for the better in all manner of different ways. However, it can also be that people are not always what they appear to be, nor as they portray themselves, and the gullible can become 'ripe pickings' for those who would love to take advantage of their simple and often too trusting natures.

Why did I turn to a medium then – albeit a spiritual medium – to seek for confirmation on my healing path? I did this, I believe, out of the sense or realisation that there is indeed guidance working in all our lives (whether we are aware of it or not), and that there are those who, through their higher level of spiritual development, are in a good position to be helpful and to give us the benefit of their advice. These are people who simply see 'deeper' than we do and who can see our own potential better than we can ourselves and who therefore have a wider and truer perspective.

Of course, as a spiritual healer I feel I am but a willing and conscious channel for healing energies directed by Spirit and the notion of spirit doctors working through healers on the earth plane is one that I have long been familiar with and which strikes me as entirely plausible (see my book, *Spirit Healing*), as does the concept of guides and helpers in Spirit. In order to make contact with such out-of-the-body friends, my wish to enlist the services of a good and reliable 'medium' seemed to me entirely reasonable.

Looking back, I feel deeply grateful that I found Anne to give me the readings that I asked for. Without asking you cannot expect to receive; I think this is a spiritual law which respects our freedom of choice. However, having asked, and received, one is then faced with how to respond and react to that which has been communicated and willingly given. Should it be accepted or rejected; believed or disbelieved? Well, here we come back to the four essentials or criteria which I identified a little earlier, and which rely on thoughtful and sensible considerations. In a nutshell, it is to use good common sense.

I found the readings I received from Anne, and which I requested at approximately monthly intervals for the first six readings, very interesting, encouraging, and confirmatory of my healing work. It was heartening to become aware of the existence of Dr John working with me and to be informed, in answer to one of my questions, that he had been doing so for about five years. This also reminded me of the second of the psychic portraits I had received from Patrick Gamble in April 2000, in which he described the person with his doctor's bag containing remedies for many ills. Could this have been Dr John already revealing his presence around me? And then, in the readings, came the additional revelation of my guide and teacher, Joshua Isaiah, and his particular role. The tone and content of what Anne wrote to me were, I felt, impressive and convincing. Nothing was to be forced upon me against my will (which, of course, I would have instinctively rejected!), but instead a cooperative way of working together, with opportunities for further development and learning were being offered to me.

Dr John had, for example, said in the third reading that he was more than willing to come to me when I sat in the silence and asked him to, and that this would be 'a more satisfactory way of communication than meeting through a medium...' To my question sent to Anne for a fourth reading about the manner of communication that could take place directly between Dr John and I, Anne wrote, 'You will be able to hear his voice in your head. Do not be impatient with this, because his thoughts will be in your voice not his.'

In the fifth reading Joshua came through to Anne to answer my questions and to make me aware that he and other guides were with me more often than Dr John. She said, 'He tells me that yes, the people around you will come through to you the same way as Dr John and you just need to be open-minded enough to start up a relationship with them.'

In the sixth reading Joshua confirmed to me once again that I had the ability to go it alone – that is, to be my own medium for his and John's and others communications: 'Bob, give heart you no longer need to utilise this medium, although I know she is more than willing to participate in your future development.'

The readings had, therefore, opened up a possibility which I had certainly not foreseen or expected, perhaps no more than I had expected Doreen Fare to tell me nearly seven years ago, and with conviction, that I could also do healing.

I had been advised by Dr John to set aside regular times for 'sitting in the silence'. Joshua had also taken the same line when, for example, he said in one of the readings:

> 'I beseech you to take the time out and sit so that we can do learning exercises together. You may feel the sitting is an inconvenience, but if you do not attend school you will not learn the lessons prepared for you.'

This point was again made by him in the eighth reading, when Anne wrote:

> He also says to keep the balance to sitting in the silence equal to the periods of sitting with mental activity, because I am being shown scales and at the moment there is more on the thinking level than on the silence side.

I had tried, it is true, to practice such regular 'sitting in the silence'. However, to keep this up was difficult and, as I write these words, I am only too aware that I have not yet managed to do this in any sustained way. In place of this, what has happened is that I can tune in, so to speak, to my friends on the other side more or less at a moment's notice. Therefore it is now the right time to describe what happens when I strike up a communication with Dr John, Joshua or, at times, with my mother who passed over nearly five years ago.

Initially, when I began to be open to receive communications, I did attempt this in times set aside for coming to as much peace and quiet in myself as I could create. I have no record or dates of these early attempts, but considering that Dr John first proposed this direct contact with him in the third reading of 10 March 2005, it is safe to assume that I was making efforts to do this during the spring of that year. The inner exercise, then, was to distinguish my own thoughts from those thoughts which came or flowed to me from another source.

I remember at one point I experimented with speaking out these thoughts verbally in order to capture them on my tape recorder. However, technically this did not work very well and the recording was poor. I tried to be receptive to receiving teachings from Joshua and sometimes also putting questions to him or John and then jotting down the gist of what was said from memory.

In the first of my notebooks, the early entries in July and September are such 'memory records'. However, towards the end of September I started to write down, as if by dictation, the thoughts which flowed into my mind when communication had been initiated by me. This has remained my preferred mode of recording my various communications ever since, that is to say, over the past six or seven months. I now have five notebooks containing these 'dictated' contents.

I should, however, hasten to point out that these writings are not the result of what is often referred to as 'automatic writing', where a medium either in a trance condition of consciousness, or perhaps, even whilst wide awake, simply allows his or her hand to be moved by the spirit entity to bring through written communications. The medium in such cases of automatic writing usually has no idea what has been written until the communication ceases and he or she, or someone else, reads back the script. This is not what happens with me and neither would I wish to cooperate in such a way of working, even assuming that such messages were of 'good quality'. No. In my case, the communications occur entirely on the mental level of clear and articulate thoughts, which I then choose to commit to paper by taking up a pen and writing them down myself.

Being a lifelong student of Rudolf Steiner's anthroposophy, I very much value clear thinking and inner freedom and would not wish to sacrifice, or perhaps even jeopardise, either of these states whilst communicating inwardly with others in this way. Neither, to make this quite clear, do I hear voices in my head. Were I to do so, I would seriously consider seeking psychiatric advice or counselling at the very least!

No, the communications I receive were and are, as described by my spirit friends, in the form of my own thoughts but not, to my knowledge or experience, of my own making or construction. In other words, telepathic communication is taking place as from mind to mind. Just in case you might be wondering if I have any other psychic abilities, such as seeing clairvoyantly those who have died, or seeing coloured energy fields and auras around people, the answer is, no, I'm afraid not.

As I have already confessed, I have not yet had the strict discipline to set up, for any sustained period, regular fixed times for these communications to take place. This, together with regular 'sitting in silence', is a challenge which still remains to be realised.

Fortunately, this has not resulted in a withdrawal of my friends' willingness to make contact with me when I ask them to draw near. Instead of meeting at fixed times in the day or week, rather like keeping a pre-arranged telephone appointment, communication can usually take place whenever I request it. Typically, this happens in the following manner.

I sit myself down in my study and have a notebook and a pen on my desk in front of me. The door is locked to avoid interruptions. I become inwardly relaxed and quiet and say some words of prayer; sometimes the Lord's Prayer. I request whoever I wish to communicate with to draw near, and I sit and wait patiently in the stillness. Usually within a few minutes I receive a very clear physical sign that my spirit friend has drawn close to me. This sign is a sudden and brief shaking of my body, which I am, by now, very accustomed to and accept as a matter of course. Almost immediately after this shaking has ceased, mental communication begins. If the communicator is Joshua, then he typically begins with his greeting word, 'Shalom', and also ends with the same greeting. ('Shalom' – which, according to the *Collins English Dictionary* is short for 'shalom aleichem' – is Hebrew and means 'peace be with you'; it is used by Jews as a greeting or farewell.)

As soon as the flow of thoughts begins, I pick up my pen and start to write, rather quickly, what is coming through rather as a secretary receives dictation. At times, especially if there is a short pause in the flow of thoughts – or perhaps through trying to coin the best word to express some meaning – my right hand and lower arm can shake somewhat. This is not a problem, and ceases as soon as the writing resumes. When the communication has been completed, the flow of thoughts will stop; it is always quite obvious and clear when we have come to the end of a particular topic or question. However, if I have another question I will ask it and await the reply, which is usually again quite quick in coming.

I have not timed these communication link-ups, but would estimate that they can vary from ten minutes to three quarters of an hour or so, depending on the reason for the contact. In the case of linking up with Joshua, I sometimes make it known that I am open and willing to receive whatever lesson or teaching he wishes to give me at that time, or else I may have specific questions which I wish to put to him. Questions to do with the healing work are normally reserved for linking up with Dr John.

As when doing healing, communicating in this telepathic way in no way makes any demands on my own energy levels; that is, I do not feel drained or tired in the least. Until very recently, I had not communicated in this way with anyone else physically present in my room. So far this has happened on just two occasions, with friends who were both aware of my ability to link up in this way with Spirit and, naturally, this took place for genuine reasons, that is, not to simply give a demonstration of communication per se but, in both cases, to put specific questions to Joshua and John. Again, only recently have I received communications intended for and requested by others: for a friend and for family members, and again for specific reasons.

Therefore, to share in the following chapters a selection of the communications which I have directly received and written down constitutes a very large step into the unknown, certainly in as much as I cannot know beforehand how you the reader will view these contents nor the sources from which, I believe, they have come. It is therefore, perhaps, a genuine leap of faith and trust on my part both in my spirit friends and also in myself.

To end a chapter called 'A Doubting Thomas' with such

A Doubting Thomas

a leap of faith and trust may appear almost ironical! However, there is no doubt that in working consciously with Spirit 'trust' is a keyword and a key faculty which needs to be developed and strengthened. Trust and confidence allow things to take place which otherwise are obstructed and stifled by distrust and doubts. The healer needs to trust in the healing energies and in his/her ability, and guidance, to channel them through to another. The medium likewise needs to trust in those in Spirit who wish to make contact with or respond to people on the physical earth plane. There is, however, I think, a difference between 'blind' faith and trust, and a faith and trust which gradually arises through experience, humility and insight. In the words from Joshua out of the eighth reading: 'Trust comes from the heart, it has nothing to do with the mental level...'

To listen to what lives and sounds in our heart is to tune in with our own soul, as the very core of our being. Is it not?

Communicating with Dr John

I would like to remind you, as I now present a small selection of the communications that have come to me from John, to bear in mind the criteria mentioned in the last chapter for judging and assessing such telepathically received contents. Namely, the motivations and intentions to altogether communicate – for example, as reflected in the sorts of questions that I have asked – and the quality and tone of the communications, as well as their actual contents. Above all, to apply the test of sound common sense as we do, hopefully, in our discourses in everyday life. Do these communications ring true to you or not?

26 September 2005

How do you feel the healing work is going, also with the children with special needs?

> Dear Bob, the healing work goes well. I am pleased with the results which you are having, although, of course, you know perfectly well that the results come through our mutual cooperation in Spirit. With regard to the work with children with special needs, this also progresses well and I want to assure you that the effects are greater than you might believe. These souls are in need of the healing you can give to them. Remember that they are, by and large, trapped in bodies that are dysfunctional in various ways and this causes a lot of frustration for them – much more than many people realise.
>
> You know, Bob, that in reality the being of the child

is soul and spirit, and that this being is trying to work into earthly life but that the limitations of the body and constitution make this, for such children, particularly difficult and painful. Therefore great sympathy and compassion and empathy are needed to do the healing work which you, and others, do. So do not belittle in any sense the importance and significance of your healing impulse with these children, even if the 'results' and outcomes are not so immediately apparent as they might be with other children or with adults.

I say this, Bob, to encourage you in your healing work with these children, because it is really important what you are doing and, in time, this will become more apparent. Patience, my friend, in all things is asked for. Patience and perseverance will in time bear rich fruits both for you and others. So feel encouraged and strengthened in your work. God bless.

11 October 2005

I asked how the work was going with particular children.

Bob, the work with P progresses well even though you may not think so from what you observe. You are building up a pattern for him and he is able to respond and absorb healing energies that he desperately needs. Be thankful that he is as receptive as he is and look forward to greater receptivity and benefit as your sessions continue.

D is very different from P yet both have the need to experience peace and security. The work with D also goes well and you have made a good relationship with this young man. In time it will bear fruit. So, once again, persevere in your healing task with him.

S very much appreciates the healings. She is well able already to come to peace and this does her much more good than even you may believe! She is the one in whom already you see the good that is being done.

Bob, I only wish to say that I am happy to be working with you and that we shall continue our work in this way. Goodnight, my friend, sleep well, and God's grace be unto you.

20 October 2005

Bob, my friend, I understand the difficulties that you describe. However, my friend, do not worry about these things. You are not perfect! None of us are – also on this side of life. We must always strive to do the best that we can under the circumstances that prevail. You are doing good work. Be assured of this, my friend. Our working together goes well and whilst it is right always to strive or wish for more, for doing better what one is doing, we must also accept our limitations and not allow these to bring about undue frustrations, or else these frustrations themselves will impede further progress.

So, my friend, let me reassure you that your/our healing work is going well, better than you might appreciate. Take heart my friend, persevere, have trust and faith in yourself and in our cooperation.

You are, of course, self-critical because you do things very consciously. This is good and right but, on the other hand, you should also relax, trust, and, yes, have a sense of humour. Keep it light, my friend. Humour is our great salvation; humour to laugh at oneself. Yes one must try hard at what one does, but one must also not take oneself too seriously! Herein lies the balance, the middle ground, the equilibrium.

I then asked John questions to do with the healing of particular adult patients, and then also the following:

Is it permissible to share these communications with patients, or better not?

Bob, it is up to you! You must be the judge of this. If you feel it's all right and in the patient's best interests, then feel free to do so. However, you also are meant to abide by the rules of your healing organisations. So our advice is 'take care', proceed slowly and with caution, but still do what you think is best. The aim is always to give maximum help and healing to individuals. Do carry on the good work, Bob. Let the healing flow. You know that I/we are working with you whenever you give healing. You almost don't need to ask, because our link is there and we know the purpose for which we are working together. God bless. John.

23 October 2005 (on the Isles of Scilly)

Bob, my friend, know that I am here with you and grateful that you wish to speak with me this evening.

My friend, the healing work goes exceedingly well! You are tuning in with me, so to speak, and are aware of my presence.

Yes, my friend, you are aware of my presence because you now take it for granted that we work together. This is what I mean to say. I do not say that you see me. I do not show myself to you; it would after all not be necessary. Although the other day you almost did see me, is that not true? You felt my presence then.

My advice to you, Bob, is to be at peace. Surrender yourself willingly to the flow of energies. Do not try too hard. That is always the problem. To try too hard sets up its own obstacles and tensions. So, my friend, just relax! Be at peace. Your part is simple; do it joyfully and confidently, and then all will be well.

I then enquired how the healing was going with a friend who had a serious ankle injury.

Bob, my friend, your work on his ankle has already done some good. He has less pain and the ankle moves easier. He will tell you this himself when you see him again. My words will be confirmed. So yes, my friend, continue to give him healing and we will do all that we can to improve his condition.

24 October 2005 (still on the Isles of Scilly)

How is the healing of J's ankle proceeding?

> Bob, good evening. You ask how J's ankle is progressing. The answer to this, my friend, is as follows.
> Progress is being made. The swelling is being reduced and the tendon is stretching. The numb part of his foot is receiving attention and feeling will slowly return there also. Please continue with your healing work with him as we wish to direct all healing energy to further his good progress.
> The injury was serious and quite complicated, but we are managing to put things aright through the contact you are making with him. I believe with this I have answered your question, Bob.

How is the healing with K?

> Bob, the healing that you have given to this lady is bearing fruit. She is more comfortable than she was and the cause of her aching joints is being remedied. We are optimistic of a successful outcome with this lady. The left knee has a particular problem that is also being addressed and healed. She will contact you again, as you arranged, and so further healings will be arranged and the good work already achieved can be furthered.

How about B?

> Your friend B is recovering well from the damage to her knuckles. You were able to initiate this healing process when you saw her last and she should make a complete recovery, also with regard to the tendons. It will, of course, take a little time, but it goes well...
> Well done, my friend, for playing your part in these healings, and may our work and cooperation grow from strength to strength as we continue to work together in trust and harmony. John.

25 October 2005 (still on Scilly)

Is it all right if I put questions to you?

> Bob, my friend, it is all right that you have questions to ask me.
> Bob, it is true that your friend experienced some increased pain after your healing session on Monday. Do not be alarmed at this. It is all part of the healing process. The injury was severe and we are doing our best to readjust and realign the tendons, muscles and ligaments that control the ankle.

Is there already an improvement with this?

> Yes, my friend, already an improvement to be seen. We shall continue our work to bring greater flexibility and movement to his affected ankle and we urge you to look for improvement through your healing efforts.

How long will it take for a complete recovery?

> Bob, it is not possible to say at this stage how long it will take for a complete recovery. Much still has to be done. Also, as you know, there is some nerve damage,

so that half his foot is numb. We are working to restore feeling and sensation there. Trust, my friend, that help is being given and healing is taking place. It is important however that your friend does not overdo his activity or strain the ankle in any way, as this would only delay improvement.

Bob, my friend, I thank you also for putting these questions and being open to receive my answers.

Good night, my friend, until we speak again. God bless.

12 November 2005

My dear friend Bob, thank you for contacting me this evening. The healings go well as you know. You know through the results that you see. This, my friend, is ample confirmation of the progress of our work together. As always the hardest task for you is to have full confidence and faith in our working together and to remove from your mind any doubts or negativity that comes towards you. Think, my friend, of the light, as Joshua has taught you. Think of this light pouring through your hands when you give the healing and going into the dark places that require healing help. The energy flows through you, my friend. You are my healing channel and I am immeasurably grateful for this as it enables me to continue my work of healing from the side of Spirit.

Yes, my friend, if you wish to ask me about particular cases, so to speak, I am happy to enlighten you as far as I am able to. Fire away!

I asked about particular adults that had been coming to see me for healing.

You know, my friend, how tricky this MS [multiple sclerosis] condition is. There is no cure for it, medically speaking. However, that does not mean that nothing can be done to alleviate or even sometimes reverse the condition which affects the nerves. In the case of A, we ask you to persevere in your treatment of her, so that there is the best chance of procuring good results. This will require much time and patience. No quick results are possible because of the very nature of the illness. But please do not give up. Persevere!

I asked about W.

In this case very good progress is being made and we have already seen a substantial improvement in the neck and the knee areas. We are working to relieve the cause of trouble in the lower back area and expect to see good results quite shortly. Thank you for facilitating this help for her.

After speaking of other cases, John had this to add.

You ask, my friend, why you so easily pick up, or rather transmit/receive, our communications. This is because you have made yourself receptive and willing to do so! For this we are truly grateful. Do not doubt the validity of this. These are true communications, as will be seen by the results you achieve. God bless, my friend, and may our work continue to prosper. John.

Most of my notes of communications with Dr John are concerned with asking questions about people to whom I was giving healing, both adults and children. To include all these accounts here would produce far too long a chapter. Already in what has been written so far the friendly and positive quality and tone of the communications shines through quite clearly. Even with continued experience in giving healing, I, for one, am often aware of my shortcomings, internal distractions, unwanted thoughts and images, and doubts, and therefore it is helpful to emphasise just how supportive, understanding, and tolerant are our friends in Spirit. I share the following for the possible benefit and help that others may also gain from John's advice to me.

6 December 2005

My dear friend, your doubts are always understandable. However, have faith! Believe in your own abilities, which are much greater than you give yourself credit for. You can do more than you think. Yes, Bob, your very thinking often stands in the way of your abilities in all realms.

Trust, my friend. Go with the flow, let it come. Do not try too hard nor question yourself so much. You are a healer, a channel for healing energies. Do it and judge by the results you obtain. Yours, John.

29 December 2005

How can I deal with disturbing, out of place, thoughts and mental images?

Yes, Bob, thank you for contacting me once again. Yes I will give you my considered advice on this pressing matter. In the first place, I fully understand the nature of these mental disturbances. This partly or even largely comes about because you are a sensitive person. Because you are very open for thoughts and vibrations in your surroundings. Therefore, my friend, there is a need to guard yourself against these disturbances.

This can be done psychically. I would advise the following. Imagine, my friend, that you surround yourself with spiritual armour. That you imagine, quite literally, putting on your armour every morning as a part of your morning routine and pattern. You must imagine/visualise this armour as invincible. That it really can and will protect you against psychic disturbances and attacks.

Imagine yourself, my friend, as a knight who dresses appropriately before going into battle. If you do this again and again – if you persevere – you will find that this strategy will bring about the desired results for you. Feel protected, Bob. You are far too exposed, far too open in some respects. You must be able to close your sensitivity to all and sundry. Bob, if you do this you will receive indeed the help that you need.

John, why do I get such awful, disturbing thoughts coming into my mind? What is the source/cause of this?

Bob, I already have explained that the principal cause of this is your own sensitivity. Yes, also because you seek for self-knowledge and are a seeker on the path. You are too conscious, too aware, too inward-looking and too aware of everything that is far from perfect in you. This cannot be avoided because of the path you have followed in your life and who you are. But, my friend, unless some check is put on these things, then there is always danger of the balance being tilted downwards one side or the other.

You know it yourself, Bob, that balance is the key to good health, on every level. Health is a state, a condition, of balance. When we are out of balance we fall ill on one level or another, whether mental, emotional, physical, or what not. Therefore, my friend, you must aim to create a balance in your life. Try to avoid all extremes. Try to aim for a happy equilibrium. If you do this then health will be the result.

Bob, you give to those who come to you for healing.

That is good and admirable. It is our work together to help in this way. But, my friend, the healer also needs help and healing! Not so?

Bob, I think that if you follow the advice I have already given you, then all will be well and you will soon see an improvement in your condition. The only other thing I would say to you is do not turn your attention to negative things or influences, whether they be originating in you or coming from without. The least attention you give to these things the better! Look for that which is positive. Create the positive. Generate the positive. Live the positive and then life will have that positive quality you so desire.

So, my friend, see how you get on and take heart. Do not lose faith in yourself or your good motives and intentions. Every person, Bob, has his or her struggles. For some this will be on the purely physical level, for others, on the emotional or mental levels and even on the spiritual levels. Every person has their own battles to fight and this is where the image of the knight and the armour comes in. This is not just an allegory, it is also a reality! So, my friend, do this and see what happens. Send those negative images and thoughts packing by not giving them access to your mind. Remember especially, put on the helmet, the helmet of truth. Good luck, my friend. God bless you and keep you and may our work continue to be blessed also. John.

And so into the New Year, 2006.

26 January 2006

Dear Bob, I am well indeed and I am also very pleased with our healing work. Your ability to transmit the healing energies is improving and this shows itself in the results you are achieving. Well done, my friend.

You have overcome your earlier doubts to a large degree and this enables the healing to flow through you unhindered and unclouded by doubts and uncertainties.

As your teacher, Joshua, has said this evening, everything depends on trust. Trust in God. Trust in Spirit. Trust in the help that you receive. The stronger you trust the more you will be able to achieve.

Yes, Bob, our work goes well and my colleagues in Spirit send you their greetings and blessings. They are grateful that they are also able to work with and through you and so further their own work of healing. Without willing channels on earth, this work and development and research would not be possible. So they send their heartfelt thanks to you, Bob, and they look forward to helping you achieve good results in your healing work. For now, my friend, I wish you well, and will continue to work with you to the best of my ability. Your friend, John.

I will bring the 'healing' chapter to a close with a quite long and very interesting communication from John, received towards the end of February.

23rd February 2006

Bob, I am here for you, my friend. What is it that you wish to ask me?

Bob, you are a healer, have no doubts about that. Therefore it is right and good if more people choose to come to you for healing.

I know, my friend, that even now you sometimes doubt your own abilities. Relax, my friend. Let the healing energies flow through you. Do less rather than more. Simply ask and trust and your patients will receive what they need; in spite of you, so to speak! Yes, my friend, you are not doing faith healing, yet have faith in your own abilities. I am more than pleased if more people seek you out as a healer. This will enable us to develop our work and reach more people. Our task, Bob, is to serve; to serve the needs that present themselves. See your task in that light and all will be well.

Healing opens up through contact with people, and if people benefit then they will send others. This, my friend, is a natural progression. So go with the flow. Follow where events lead you and your healing will work wonders – or rather our healing. Have courage to say 'yes' to what comes and be willing to do what is asked for. The help you need will come from Spirit. This is spirit healing...

Yes, Bob, you are quite right. It is a team and we are a part of it. Many people are involved in healing. There are specialists on our side of life as on yours. But over here they can gain greater insights and knowledge as to what are the real causes of illness and disease. This is more than treating symptoms. This is real healing. Your part is essential. We need healers through whom to channel the energies. Without this human link our work is greatly diminished. We need you and others to transmit the energies right on to the physical level.

You ask who else is involved. Well, my friend, there are many involved at this time. Those that know about hearts, eyes, ears, different organs, etc. Yes, my friend, the body is a whole but it is extremely complicated. That is why specialisms exist. But be assured all work for the same goal, to relieve suffering and pain; to do all in their power to bring comfort and ease in place of discomfort and pain. Yes, my friend, illness has a meaning in a person's life, this is true. But this does not mean that we should not do everything we can to help and to heal. This is our task, Bob, and I thank you for playing your part in this. Keep up the good work. You are being used effectively and more than you realise. Have faith, my friend. All blessings. John.

In the next four chapters we will read most of the teachings that I have, so far, received in my communications with Joshua Isaiah.

Communicating with Joshua (I)

Whereas John was primarily with me for spiritual healing, Joshua was, and is, there for teaching, learning, and development. With the communications from and with Dr John, it was only possible to give a certain selection from my notebooks. However, with the teachings received from Joshua, a nearly complete reproduction will be given in these next chapters. Just as in the readings from Anne, I firstly became aware of the existence of Dr John (actually from the very first reading), and only later of Joshua's connection with me, so in my own telepathic communications Joshua's teachings followed on from John's input on the healing work.

As I have previously explained, to begin with I simply wrote down in my notebook what I remembered of my inner communications with John and Joshua. Only several months later did I decide that it was better, more complete and accurate, to write down verbatim what I was directly receiving as thoughts. However, because of the interesting information given to me early on by Joshua, I will also include some of the rather bitty 'memory-based' communications at the beginning of this chapter. So, as one of my special needs patients says when we start a healing session, 'Here we go, then!'

3 July 2005

In responding to my question concerning our relationship in previous lives, he referred to an incarnation in Ancient Egypt in which I painted pictures/signs on temple walls. [Also, in answer to a recent query from me since about healing, Joshua explained that I was a doctor in a much later incarnation, not the one in Ancient Egypt.]

9 July 2005

I put various questions.

Was he (Joshua) really an independent being rather than a creation of myself (fantasy/imagination)?

Yes, he is an independent being, as is John. He referred to my initiative and freedom in our communication – no coercion or imposition. The physical world is illusory; behind the illusion of matter are beings and energy.

In Joshua's world – the fifth dimension – light, energy and beings are not separated in the same way as on earth.

His work? Giving teaching, understanding, and knowledge.

10 July 2005

I asked about whether our communication/contact could also be for the benefit of others and not just of personal value.

The answer was that it can/will be of value to others if I communicate this by word of mouth or perhaps by writing (a book) as others have done before. This helps to build the bridge, to make people aware of the reality of the connection between the different dimensions of existence, between Spirit and our earthly world.

I asked for help for those killed in the bombs in London and Joshua said that much help was being given. Some people would not realise that they had 'died', and a gentle awakening to life on the other side was needed.

I asked about the gift of clairvoyance, in addition to clairaudience. The answer, as before, is to be patient. Gifts are given when one is ready. The timing for such things cannot be said.

John – greetings given and healing requested.

23 July 2005

The teaching to value earthly life. The uniqueness of the opportunities for growth and development that life on earth provides. Therefore, again and again souls seek re-embodiment. Seek the family, the parents, the environment, to fulfil their destiny and karma. The tragedy of suicide, of giving up. Value earthly life.

Courage is needed to say, 'Yes, yes, yes.' To meet what life brings and make the most of it.

This is the lesson for tonight.

3 September 2005

I put certain questions to Joshua:
Do you link up/teach others as well as myself?

> Yes, as you suspect, I link with others also, since my task is to be a teacher giving knowledge and insights into Spirit.

The link we have you said before originated in a previous incarnation. Can you say more about this?

> Yes, we were on earth in Ancient Egypt. You had the task of painting pictures of the gods in the tombs and were also linked with healing. I was then also a teacher in the Mysteries. But we were linked also in Greek/Roman times.

A friend of mine (H S) referred to our (hers and mine) connection in the Grail Stream. Is this correct?
[I had met H S whilst attending Emerson College in 1973 in Sussex, and felt that I knew her already – from a previous lifetime. On my visits to her flat she would tell me, full of wonder and enthusiasm, of Parsifal and his quest for the Holy Grail. She once gave me a book called *Guidance*

in Esoteric Training by Rudolf Steiner and wrote inside it: 'To Bob, fellow pioneer pilgrim – so happy we've met on our Karmic path this time.' She also wrote to me these words: 'If we do not meet for a day, a month, a year, a lifetime, what of it? The link has been forged. Aye, even beyond death, and so we hail and recognise each other when destiny decrees and Evolution brings it round again to further its great Aims on its Laws. But we also shall have the personal joy of the Karmic recognition – reunion of soul and spirit as Knights on the Grail Path Brotherhood.']

> Yes, this was correct and later you also had your incarnation as a monk in a non-speaking Order.

I also asked about the genuineness of this communication with Joshua, since I still found this rather amazing. I linked up again in the morning and asked further questions about this; my ability for this; the question of the guardian of the threshold; distinguishing truth from illusion; and received answers but did not record them.

10 September 2005

The teachings given were about:

- hindrances and obstacles as opportunities and aids on the path of development;
- relationships based on mutual care and respect;
- tolerance – not imposing one's own views on others; and
- relationships on various levels – spiritual, mental, emotional, physical, sexual – all have their rightful place.

I put a question regarding my development/progress as a healer.

You know the answers yourself, through the results of your healing work. Yes, indeed the answers to all your questions are in your own heart/self/spirit. Listen to your heart.

We can help you to find the keys to your own wisdom.

It is not the quantity but the quality that matters. Practice the linking up, which is easy and can be made to others also.

Greetings from Dr John.

The first two fully 'dictated' communications from Joshua that I wrote down were received in October as given below and were very much Michaelmas teachings, some of which I even dared to share with a few friends for the first time.

1 October 2005

Shalom, my friend. Peace be with you. At this time in your world there is much tribulation and suffering. These things must be if change – real change – is to come about. We do not wish to bring about suffering of any kind – this is not our intention – but, my friend, you must realise that it is often only through pain and suffering that ears will open and messages be received.

The world must change, the power of love must be felt and for this to happen great changes are needed to purge and cleanse much that has become rotten and evil.

You think of Michaelmas, my friend, and rightly so, because only by uniting with the Spirit can real hope be found in your world. The age of materialism must pass and a new spiritual awakening must dawn – St Michael's Dawn, you may rightly say.

So, my friend, be not perturbed by all that happens to bring about change. Many things must take place if the new is to establish itself and replace the old order.

People generally do not want change, not change in their lives and lifestyles. Yet without fundamental changes the world cannot move forward – the Christ Age cannot prevail.

He died for our sins, yes, but we must play our part in transforming the globe. This is an age of freedom. There must be choice, but wise choice is not always made. So my teaching tonight, my friend, is to take heart; do not become downcast at all the horrors of this world. See them as the necessary preparation for better times to come. To come, that is, if human beings *will* them to come, in freedom and love.

Shalom, my friend. May God's blessing be with you, and may he keep you safe from harm.

8 October 2005

Shalom, my friend. Thank you once again for making contact with me by again taking the initiative, because you know that this contact is dependent on your own free will. I will not impose myself upon you.

Yes, my friend, I do have teaching to give you this evening and I thank you for making this transmission possible.

You see around you in the world great disasters on every hand. There are shocking experiences and this, my friend, is just the point. These experiences are given to shock humanity to awakeness – to waken out of the sleep of the material world – to awaken to the Spirit.

We know how painful this is. We know what sufferings are entailed for so many people. Yet, my friend, these are the signs of the times. Without these shocks, humanity will continue to dream its life away. The Spirit knocks on the door, and the door must be opened. But to open this door needs courage and will; it cannot be opened otherwise. The time is at hand.

Hearts should awaken; minds should see and hear what the Spirit speaks. This is why these shocks and disturbances are taking place in the earth and in the air and wind and water. The very elemental world wants humanity to wake up. These things must come to pass. Without them the sleep of earth existence goes on and on and man will lose his spirit knowledge. This is the teaching, the message I give you tonight, my friend. I give my love and blessing to you. Shalom, my friend. Peace be with you, and I thank you again for receiving this teaching. Joshua.

Then on a more personal note.

11 October 2005

Shalom, my friend. Yes, in answer to your question, you can indeed develop further, much further in fact, your own powers of conscious mediumship. And you can do this in the realm of pure thought as is your inclination and wish. And I can help you in this regard, provided this is what you truly want. Remember, my friend, there is never any compulsion or obligation from the side of Spirit for you to develop your powers. This is your own free choice. If you make this choice in favour of developing your mediumship in addition to your healing powers, then we will help you willingly to do so.

Yes, my friend, your powers once developed can indeed be put to good use to help others. Indeed, as you say, what otherwise is the point?

Yes, Bob, what you did in sharing this teaching [the Michaelmas ones], was right. It sprang from a genuine impulse to share what you had received and not simply keep it to yourself. Of course, what others will make and do with such a sharing you cannot guarantee or know. That rests with them. Nevertheless, the wish to share what you had received from Spirit was a right motive and impulse. Well done, my friend, for having the courage to do this.

I put a question to Joshua about the source of these thoughts. Could fantasy, wishful thinking, play a part in this?

Bob, you know that this is not the case. We have told you this before, but nonetheless we understand your doubts and questions. You are, after all, a thinker. But trust yourself, my friend. Trust is the keyword, which you yourself wrote! Is it not so?

Yes my friend, if your questions are specifically to do with healing then I would advise you to speak to Dr John directly. Remember that he also works with a team of doctors and healers and therefore they are in the best position to answer your specific healing questions. However, other questions that you have can be addressed directly to me since my task is precisely to help you to learn and to grow and to develop your knowledge and insights.

Shalom, my friend. Yes you can also receive messages from angels. It would be communicated in different ways, depending on your need. Remember, my friend, God works in mysterious ways his plan to fulfil. The angels are always with us, in life and death; that is, in Spirit. Remember also that the name 'angel' means messenger; so a major task of the angels is precisely that: to give messages to those in need. But as I have said, these messages can come through in different ways.

I then went on to speak with Dr John about healing matters.

The communications that follow are once again very

personal in content, and I wondered whether to include them in this book or not. I have decided to do so because they clearly illustrate the relationship between Joshua and me, and also something of my own astonishment and continued questioning of such communications.

13 October 2005

I asked Joshua if I could enquire about my previous incarnations.

> Shalom, my friend. Yes you can certainly ask such questions and I am permitted to give you answers.
>
> Bob, in your previous incarnation you were a monk, a monk in a non-speaking Benedictine Order. You lived in France, the very place that in this life you feel no connection with, and the reasons for this are certain painful and difficult experiences you had in that incarnation at the hand of the Inquisition. You were tortured, my friend, and had to undergo great hardships. Something of this has thrown a shadow into your present life, though by now it is behind you.
>
> You died when you were forty-three years old. It was a sudden death at the hand of your torturers.
>
> You became a monk when you were eighteen years old and you had always wished to serve God in this way. You were devoted to the life in the monastery and had many friends then – good friends. One of them was H whom you met and knew at once in this life. She was then a man, your teacher and superior in the monastery. You had a close, a very close connection, a connection of love in a true sense. This is, of course, the reason why when meeting her again in your present life there was an instant recognition and attraction.

I asked Joshua about my parents.

> Yes, Bob, there were connections indeed. Your parents in this present life were also with you in an earlier incarnation. They served you then also out of love and friendship. So you see, my friend, how love spans lifetimes!
>
> Yes, my friend, you were a healing monk; you had actually then the gift of healing and helping. This you felt a special calling to do and this was allowed in your Order. You learnt it from H, your friend and tutor; she taught you how to heal. Yes, my friend, all this may sound far-fetched to you but true it is. In that lifetime she was versed in the magic arts, but out of high moral purposes and these she passed on to you.
>
> So your task, my friend, was as a healer monk, helping the sick and ill. This was your task then.
>
> You died young because you were considered to blaspheme. Not that you did, I hasten to add. You were true to your calling, but not in the eyes of the Inquisition. Your very Order was regarded as heretical and blasphemous in the eyes of the Holy Church authorities. My friend, it is as well that you have no memory of your torture and death.

Where did I live?

> Near Lyons, my friend, in Southern France. Look for it on a map and you will find it there. This is where the Order was based and here you lived the greater part of your life. Now do you understand, my friend, why France has always been a hole in your mind? It has to do with the difficult experiences you underwent in that incarnation, that lifetime.
>
> I have answered the question you put and perhaps you feel that that is enough for tonight? Are you to

believe all this? Well my friend, here you must make
up your own mind, but I have told you what is true.
Your friend and teacher in Spirit, Joshua Isaiah.

In 1998 I received an auragraph – an aura drawing which I had requested from William Lambert, who has the faculty to perceive auras. It was accompanied by a tape recording made whilst he drew my aura. In it at one point he refers to me being a monk in my previous incarnation; a monk belonging to a non-speaking Order. In my twenties I visited Prinknash Abbey in Gloucestershire with the thought of perhaps going there, for a retreat at least. I spoke there to a monk of the Benedictine Order – a tall, dignified looking man – but I felt that what I was looking for could not be found in a monastery after all.

France is, for me, a peculiar non-entity in my geography of Europe.

15 October 2005

Shalom, my friend. Yes I am here once again to be with you, as I always am, and to help you to gain in understanding, knowledge, and wisdom.

I want to ask further about my previous incarnations. Is this a valid question to ask?

Yes, Bob, it is valid to ask these questions, because through knowledge of earlier lives you also gain insights and direction and guidance for your present and future lives.

Yes, my friend, you have lived many times before and done many different things in these lives. Some you would now be happy with, but others not so!

To learn, we need to pass through many different learning experiences, joys and sorrows.

You wonder, my friend, about your life in Ancient Egypt and this was, in truth, a fascinating time and culture.

I have already told you that you were engaged in decorating the tombs of kings and pharaohs. I have told you also that at that time I was your teacher. Know, my friend, that we have been linked in many incarnations.

Yes, now you know me through this contact, but before we lived together on earth at the same time.

Here, Joshua told me to, 'Slow down, my friend; don't try too hard – relax – and let the thoughts flow.'

Yes, now you are calmer, the thoughts will still flow but without so much nervous activity!

In Ancient Egypt we were linked like teacher to pupil; almost father to son. The link was strong; I was able to give you teachings then which opened your eyes to the Spirit. The spirit world was open to your gaze, and you learnt many things of importance.

Your work was also one of healing. Not as a doctor or physician, but as someone skilled in magical arts and rituals. Yes, my friend, you may find these things difficult to believe or accept now but nonetheless, in that former time, they were so. You were able to help many people in these ways, and the sick and the suffering came to you with their troubles and you were able to do much good. You wonder, my friend, if not your own fantasy is making up stories! This is not the case I can assure you.

You worked in the Temple of Isis. You served the Goddess of Life, and within the temple walls you learnt many secrets unknown to ordinary folk. Your knowledge was great in those former days, almost like that of an Initiate. Yet I was your teacher so that, as you can imagine, my knowledge was still greater than yours.

Remember, my friend, that those who have knowledge also have much responsibility. No you didn't abuse or misuse your responsibilities. You treated them with due reverence and caution, I am glad to say.

It was, my friend, a very fruitful and important incarnation for you, and also for me. As you know from your study of Steiner's work, Ancient Egypt was a time linked to the present stage of world history. This is why you have wanted to ask about it, and this is why I also have responded to your request.

Yes, my friend, you were married and you had seven children! Yes, you had your hands full, so to speak! However, you also had slaves in your household to attend to your family's needs.

My friend, this is not wishful thinking, however much you may think it is. The messages you receive are indeed transmitted from me, your spirit teacher.

Trust, my friend. This is for you an important lesson. You are a thinker and so you doubt. Have you not often doubted yourself again and again? Overcome this doubt, my friend. Open up your heart and let your higher self ray down. I respect your true self and I respect your self in this life. My words are given in answer to your questions. Be careful therefore, my friend, what questions you ask, lest the answers shock and surprise you!

But know that we work for the good of humanity and the world. This is the criterion and this is the measure; this is the test and the task. St Paul said, 'Test the spirits', and he was right. Doubt has its place. But when doubt has been exorcised, let trust and confidence take its place.

My friend, you have already received quite a lot from me this evening; much to think on and contemplate. The important thing is the link, my friend – the contact and the working together – to build this up. This we are doing whenever you take the initiative to bring about this contact.

> Shalom, my friend. God's blessing be with you until we speak again. Your friend in Spirit, Joshua Isaiah.

In reading through and writing out these communications from my notebooks, I am surprised by all that was given to me from Joshua. In answer to my questions, much of it is of a highly personal nature, yet have we not all lived many lives before in diverse settings and in relationships with people, some of whom we meet again in our present life? In this sense the reader may, I hope, find the communications that are shared here of some real interest. Anyway, I trust you are not bored, but can also learn something from what Joshua has imparted to me. With your interest also in mind I will continue.

23 October 2005 (on the Isles of Scilly)

> Shalom, my friend. Thank you for once again making contact with me in order to receive teaching from Spirit.
>
> I am aware that you have been reading about the teachings of White Eagle, who is indeed a teacher in the great White Brotherhood. His teachings are both pure and wise and it is good that you feel drawn towards them because much can be learnt from the simplicity and purity of his words.
>
> You ask, my friend, if I have something specific to impart to you this evening. Indeed I have and it is this.
>
> In your world at the present time you see much hardship and suffering taking place in all quarters. This is painful to the extreme. Floods, fire, wind, and weather, put many people to the test. The earth shakes and moves underfoot. All is in a state of flux and change. And this, my friend, is here to help human beings change their ways; to raise their sights, so to speak, towards the Spirit and away from matter. These are stressful and painful days. Yet they must come to

pass if humanity is to awaken from the sleep of matter and worldly desires. We in Spirit suffer with you, with all souls who go through such hardships and deprivations, especially little children. But know, my friend, that these things are there for a purpose, a greater purpose and plan which must be fulfilled.

In time, many will come to understand and see what is happening and why. As yet the eyes of many are darkened, and fear and anxiety plague many souls. But you, my friend, in receiving this message shall know the true purpose and meaning of these fateful events. Yes, my friend, you are able to know and understand these things because you are a worker for the light – a light worker. As such, you are one of many such light workers and through you, and others, clarity and knowledge can be given. Therefore, my friend, if you feel the impulse to share your knowledge and understanding please do so, but only as you see fit. One does not throw pearls to swine. In saying this you know what I mean. It is said out of respect for the truth, not out of disregard for human needs.

This, my friend, was the message, the teaching, which I specifically wanted to give you this evening. If you have questions which you wish to ask me then please feel free to do so.

I put a question about disturbing thoughts.

Shalom, my friend. Yes, I well understand your question about mental distractions and disturbances. It is, of course, not a new question! It is something that you experience on a daily basis.

Rest assured, my friend, that you are not singular in this respect. Many people experience unrest in their life of thoughts and thought images. But you, my friend, as a sensitive – as a medium, I may say – are especially conscious of your inner life and so any imperfections strike you with more force than with many others. Think of it in this way, my friend. You have a TV set and it can pick up many stations, signals, and transmissions. In a similar way, because of your sensitivity, you are also subject to many impressions, thoughts, images, that surround you. Therefore you experience much that is unpleasant to you and which puzzles you. Do not worry, my friend. Concentrate on the good that you try to do. Do not let the other unsavoury things distract you from the work you are upon: God's work. Develop your gifts, of healing, mediumship, and put them to good use for the sake of others – in service. This is all that matters.

I asked a question about Joshua's separate identity. Was he really only a part of myself or simply my wishful thinking, fantasy, etc?

Yes, my friend, I can answer this question for you. I am indeed separate from yourself and a spirit being in my own right, just as you are also a spirit being. Spirit is the reality, matter is illusion.

The thoughts you receive in communication with me are inspired into you through your mind and nervous system. I am a teacher in Spirit; this is my task. I teach you and also others who are open and receptive to my influence and contact. You know that this is done in freedom and in respect for your wishes and consent. Nothing is ever imposed or forced. Indeed you would not wish it otherwise.

I asked how Joshua experiences angels.

Shalom, my friend. I experience the angels as great beings of light and love, as true messengers of the Godhead.

I asked why my hand shakes prior to writing these communications.

> My friend, your hand shakes because you are transmitting my energy when you receive these communications. My energy impinges and inter-reacts with your own energies and nervous disposition.

I asked if I am permitted to ask questions about reincarnation and karma.

> Yes, my friend, you are permitted to ask questions to do with reincarnation and karma, because I am here to help and to teach you on your path of knowledge and understanding.

I asked if I was linked with my wife in a previous incarnation.

> Yes, my friend, you were indeed related to each other in previous earthly lives, though, of course, you have no memory of these.
>
> You were related to your wife in Ancient Greece. You were then a man of high renown and your wife was a slave. My friend, you have asked the question and I give you the answer even if you find it hard to accept or believe. But so it was.
>
> The relationship was a good one. You did treat her with kindness and respect. You lived in Athens in a rich house and setting. Your wife came from Egypt then and was the daughter of a nobleman. Although she was a slave in your household, you recognised her noble birth and background and treated her accordingly. So, my friend, you have nothing to feel ashamed about in your previous relationship with your present wife.
>
> But here you see, my friend, how your paths have

come together again and brought you into relationship as man and wife, as husband and wife. Are not the ways of the Spirit weird (maybe 'strange' would be better) and wonderful! My friend, I used the words with respect, though I admit they could be misconstrued!

Well, I think my wife, reading this for the first time, as I show her my notebook before including this personal information in this chapter, may well agree with the weird, if not wonderful, turn of phrase. She might even think that not much has changed from that lifetime to this!

I then asked Joshua about how well we are working together.

My friend, our working together goes well. Yes you are receiving the communications clearly and in your own mind, and yes it does come through to you clearly and I am aware that you are taking care to not let your own thoughts censor or disrupt the messages that are given by me. I thank you for this, my friend. The communication becomes easier with practise and also as you build up your trust and confidence in our relationship. I thank you once again for this. Without a pupil a teacher has no purpose. The teacher relies on his pupil, and I also rely on you, my friend. You enable me to communicate teachings to you, and this is the nature of our relationship.

I asked how this has come about.

This has come about my friend through our association in previous earthly lives – in Egypt, in Greece, and elsewhere.

I asked where.

> In Babylonia, in Assyria, in China, in East Asia. Many lives, my friend; many incarnations. A long association. This is why I can speak to you so freely, so easily, now that you have opened your mind and heart to the spirit realm.

Do you understand that I still find all these things quite difficult to accept?

> Yes, my friend. I understand even now the difficulties you have in accepting these teachings as truth. Therefore I say to you, test them out; listen to them. Write them down and think and ponder on them. It is not unhealthy to question these things. Indeed, it is far better than blind faith. So yes, my friend, I do understand your situation and it matters not to me, in the sense that it does not distract us from continuing our discourse.
>
> Yes, my friend, you are right. To come to peace; to be thankful and grateful for all that life brings us: it is all learning. Learning never stops, not in your world or ours. So I send my greetings and blessings to you, my friend. I am ever grateful for your friendship and your help. Take care. Shalom. Joshua.

With this sense of gratitude and thankfulness in mind, we will give ourselves a well-deserved break by bringing this chapter to a close and then, refreshed again, open ourselves to more of Joshua's teachings in the next chapter. As I warned you already, what I have received from Joshua is quite extensive and yet I am reluctant to cut it short and prevent readers from having enough material – both of quantity and quality – to help you form considered views about all this.

Communicating with Joshua (II)

Sometimes the teachings given by Joshua can appear repetitive in that the same essential points are reiterated. Where this is the case, it does not require much imagination to realise that the points made are considered by him sufficiently important to warrant repeating and to give us another opportunity to really take them to heart.

24 October 2005

Have you any teaching to give me this evening please?

> Shalom, my friend. Thank you once again for being ready to receive my teaching. It is this:
> You are disturbed by the troubles in the world. The news is full of disasters on every hand. You ask yourself why, oh why, humanity is troubled by all these things. The answer, my friend, lies in the state of humanity itself. Much has to be learnt. Tests and trials have to be undergone in order that true progress can be made. There is, I'm afraid, no other way but through hardships and traumas, that men can come to themselves – can realise their true potential. Yes, my friend, it is at times depressing to see all that must be gone through. The heart can sink. But take heart because the goal is worth it! The goal of true human achievement. The goal of a better world.
> On every hand things can go wrong. Misdeeds are done and enacted, both on the small and large scale, but remember, my friend, that this is a school of learning, and learning involves hardship. True learning is not easy. So, my friend, with this message, this

teaching, I encourage you to see through the darkness to the light, to the greater purposes which are being fulfilled at this time. Have confidence in the Spirit, in the Spirit that loves and guides all humanity. This Spirit will not let you down. It is His Will that all will be well. Trust, my friend. Trust builds the bridge. Trust is the key to know God.

This is the teaching that I wanted to give to you this evening. Shalom, my friend. God bless. Take care. Joshua.

After this I wanted to ask Joshua another question: was I making sufficient progress spiritually?

Shalom, my friend. Yes you are making progress on your spiritual path even though you may think that you are not! Persevere, my friend. It is not possible for you to see or know truly the progress that you yourself make. However, you are making progress, be assured of that. Let it happen naturally, my friend, at its own pace. Do not attempt to force matters in any way. Trust that all that is needed is happening with you and that higher powers are watching over you. With this I have answered your question.

Your friend and teacher in Spirit. Joshua Isaiah.

I have included this answer to my personal question about spiritual progress, as also with responses to other quite personal matters, purely in the hope that others may be able to benefit from Joshua's wisdom and his wider perspectives on things.

25 October 2005 (on the Scilly Isles)

Shalom, my friend. I am happy to be here with you once again and I look forward to hearing your questions.

Regarding my mediumship?

> My friend, your capacity to speak with and listen to those in Spirit has come about for you at this time because you have proved yourself ready for this. Have you not been striving inwardly for many years now? Have you not endeavoured to find the bridge to spirit worlds? Yes, my friend, you have indeed done so. You are truly a seeker for the Spirit. And so it has been granted you to realise the capacity to open your heart and mind to those in Spirit. You have, of course, been guided in this direction, and your medium friend has been instrumental in helping you to find your way. However, you now realise that it is not necessary for you to make use of the medium; you yourself are a medium in your own right.
>
> Having said this, my friend, it is up to you whether you choose to exercise this power, this ability, and to do so also for the good of others. This lies in your own hands. Never do we impose ourselves upon you. The choice is yours. Nonetheless, you have the gift that you have now discovered in yourself and we are pleased about this. Shalom, my friend.

When I was walking around the Garrison today, I tried to communicate with my mother and father who are in Spirit. How was this?

> Shalom, my friend. What took place today was indeed a reality. An important reality and of benefit to those in Spirit. It is not easy for those living in the realm of light and life and truth and wisdom, to find human souls on earth who are open and willing instruments for their messages and communications. Therefore, my friend, I can assure you that it was real what took place today and that it was important for all concerned.

Can I develop my mediumistic capacities further?

Yes, my friend, of course you can develop these capacities further if you so wish. The choice is yours!

Why me?

Why not, my friend?
Yes you are right; you are aware of many imperfections and blemishes in your own soul, but ask yourself this, my friend. Can we wait until we are perfect before we do something to help? If so we would all be waiting for a very long time! No, we must act; we must do the best that we can with what we already have and, at the same time, endeavour – strive – to improve and perfect ourselves.

My friend, be grateful for what has been given to you. Be grateful for the gift that unfolds in your soul, and show your gratitude by making good use of it for the benefit and comfort of others.

Should I become a practicing medium?

My friend, whether you should put into practice your mediumship in the way that you have asked is again up to you. I cannot tell you what to do. This is not my business; not my task.

Wait and see, my friend, what opportunities come towards you and then decide how you will act. Whatever you do should be dedicated to the service of the good and the true. Let this be your measure, your yardstick.

Can I contact other friends in Spirit?

My friend, you can contact other friends in Spirit if they also wish to have contact with you. Never impose yourself on others against their will or wish. What you did today to invite others to draw close, that is permissible, but in all matters take care and tread carefully.

Do you still have any teachings to bring through?

My friend, your questions shall suffice for tonight. I thank you for making contact with me and send you God's blessing and love. Shalom, my friend. Take care. Joshua.

The next entry in my notebook with Joshua is in November, the month in which people often think about and remember their so-called 'dead'.

12 November 2005

Shalom, my friend. Thank you for once again making contact with me. It is good to be with you once again though, in truth, I am always with you as your guide and helper.

Yes, I have teaching to give you this evening. My friend, you see many troubles happening in your world on every hand. These things must come to pass before a new age can dawn – not only dawn, but be realised.

Many changes are taking place at this time. The earth is being shaken, and those who live upon her, in order that they may also be changed. Without change there is no progress or evolution, both in a physical and a spiritual sense. And so, my friend, do not lose heart when you are aware of much that is destructive and negative around you. Believe only that all leads to good. There is no light without dark, no good without evil, no joy without sorrow, no achievement without disappointment and failure.

But all this forms part of the great plan of life –

God's plan which is to be fulfilled and realised upon Mother Earth. It is always important to be aware of this broader, wider picture, my friend. Why do I give you this teaching yet again? Because, my friend, it is so important to realise what is taking place at this point of time. To see through the murk and gloom towards the greater light that shines down into your earth plane. God's light never ceases to radiate to human beings on earth, but all depends on them turning themselves towards the light; being willing and ready to receive the light.

Christ came to bring this light to earth in human form. He is with you still, as you realise, and He it is to whom you and all human beings can turn for comfort, help, and succour. Christ is ever merciful, his love knows no bounds; his forgiveness is infinite. This is the One who brings salvation and redemption to the earth planet and the One who is most exalted amongst the gods on high. We who work for the light know of His power and love. We work with them to bring light, love, and healing to earth. We know, because we have also lived on earth, what terrible struggles you have to undergo on this plane. To be incarnated in the body, in the flesh, is to lose sight of the Light of the world and the Light of heaven, and yet it is, of course, through Christ that this light is revealed to you. God reveals Himself through his Son, his only begotten Son.

It is so important, my friend, that others, like yourself, are aware of these realities. That others, like yourself, turn towards the Spirit to seek knowledge and wisdom. We are here to inspire you, to teach you, to help you understand the situation in which you find yourselves, even when it seems most dark and dismal. Trust in us, my friend. We are here to help – to help in every way we are permitted – for, as you know, all depends on man's free will. We are not allowed to impose or force ourselves on others against their wishes or will. Therefore it is such a joy when one among you is open to receive our teachings and help.

Shalom, my friend, this is the teaching I wished to send through you this evening and I thank you for permitting this to take place. Now have you any further questions for me?

Why do I experience such difficulties in my own thought life?

My friend, you are experiencing these things because you are a light worker. Only because you strive for the light do you also become aware of the dark, both within and without.

Take heart, my friend. What happens on the bigger scale – all that I have just described to you – also takes place on the smaller scale within yourself.

Yes it is like a battleground, this is true, but it is a battle with meaning and purpose. It is a struggle through which you can grow strong and stronger still. Above all do not lose sight of the light – the living light that is within you. Do not allow yourself, my friend, to be distracted or upset by these other things. They must be; they assail you just because you make progress on your spiritual path. Were you not striving, they would not present as such a problem. These things are sent to test us. Do not forget this. Be true to yourself, my friend; take heart, ask God for his boundless help and all will be well.

Shalom, my friend. Peace be with you. Joshua Isaiah.

As the reader will be more than aware by now, I experience my greatest tests, and challenges, on the mental plane in the realm of thoughts and mental images. The reason why I share Joshua's advice about how to deal with these things is quite simply because I believe this advice may also be helpful to others. I don't think I am alone in having these sorts of experiences. Everyone will have their own 'inner landscape' containing both positive and negative, pleasant and unpleasant, beautiful and ugly, images and thoughts. They can lead sometimes to joy, inspiration, and peace with oneself and, at other times, also to despair and inner turmoil and disquiet. In the second reading I received from Anne, in which I also sought advice about distracting, unwanted thoughts, Anne remarked:

> He [Dr John] is telling me the unwanted thoughts are a problem that 99.9% of people have, and that it is only through training the mind and relaxation that the mind can learn not to attach to these thoughts; this will control the problem.

Back to Joshua.

24 November 2005

Shalom, my friend. Yes I am quite agreeable that you ask me questions this evening if that is your wish. I will endeavour to answer your questions to the best of my limited ability.

My dear friend, the thoughts and images which trouble you are sent to test you. To test your trust in the Spirit world and to test your faith in yourself. Tests come in many different shapes and forms. For you it is on this mental level. You must learn, my friend, to ignore and defuse these unwanted thoughts and images, to relegate them to the place where they belong – give them to the world ether to dissolve and evaporate.

I understand how troubling these things are for you. It is always so when one strives for the Spirit, that such tests and challenges are presented. Do not be downcast or disheartened. You can overcome these obstacles by not giving them undue weight or importance. Treat them for what they are worth: next to nothing. After all, they do not represent in any shape or form your true aspirations; just the opposite, in fact. So, my friend, ignore them as much as possible, do not encourage them in any way, then you will be free of their distracting power. Be true to yourself, not to these unwanted and troublesome things.

About my mediumship?

Shalom, my friend. Yes, you have indeed mediumistic abilities or else you would not be receiving these communications right now! However, I well understand that you feel you could not give public demonstrations such as you witnessed this evening.

[He is referring here to an evening of 'clairvoyance' I had attended in which a medium gave messages to some of those who had come to this public event.]

That is fine – no one is asking you to do this. These demonstrations are valuable and important for those who gain solace, encouragement and enlightenment through them. It is not, however, your way. Your mediumistic abilities can be used, however, for giving messages of a higher order, if we may put it like that. I mean messages, information, knowledge, which flows from higher regions of Spirit. This ability can develop further if you wish to do so, and we will help you to do this if you ask for it. Remember, my friend, you are bringing through messages on the pure thought level, not on the level of feelings and emotions.

Do you have anything to say to me this evening?

> Yes, my friend, I would like to share with you the following. We in Spirit are working hard to establish relations and communication with those on earth. To do this, we need to find human beings who are open and receptive and willing to act as channels and receivers of our thoughts. This is a task which you have begun to take on and we would wish to encourage you to persevere with this. Where it will lead to will be revealed in due course, but it is important that such work can take place. For this my friend, we thank you and send you all blessings from Spirit, from the realms of light and love. Shalom, my friend. God bless. Yours, Joshua Isaiah.

29 November 2005

Shalom, my friend. It is good to make contact with you again though, truth be told, I am never far away from you.

You ask if I have anything to communicate to you. Yes I have. I wish to tell you something of the progress you are making, as I recognise that you need reassurance at times. My friend, you have made good progress even if you are not aware of it yourself. Your abilities for healing and communication are progressing well and steadily, and this is by far the best way. Slow and steady progress is much preferred to leaps and bounds!

Remember, you receive what you need and also what you can manage. Spiritual evolution is a long process. It cannot be hurried and rushed. Trust in God; trust in those powers that guide and help you, and you will continue along the path which is destined for you – the path you yourself have chosen. Healing is a great gift, a gift of God; make full use of it, my friend, as you are doing at present, and do not be disheartened if you do not achieve immediate results. You are now seeing some people with chronic long-lasting conditions, and these conditions need time and patience to heal. Do not be discouraged, but persevere as John has asked you to. Remember that you are working as part of a team – a much bigger team than you may imagine. But we/they are not miracle workers! Healing is an exact science, and it follows certain laws and methods. Trust, my friend, that you are indeed receiving the help that you need and that you can pass this help on to others. Trust, trust, trust, is the keyword. In this way you will remove all obstacles to the healing flow.

Shalom, my friend. This is the teaching I give you this evening, which will help you on your way; on your path as a healer. Goodnight, my friend. God bless. Shalom. Peace. Joshua Isaiah.

Into December and on the way to Christmas.

6 December 2005

Shalom, my friend. Thank you for communicating with me once again. I fully understand that you need to be in the right mood to do this work. Do not worry about this. Accept what is possible for you. To force things is of no help. Simply be grateful that, at times, you can make this link and receive these communications.

I must have asked questions then, but failed to write them down; but I have the replies as follows.

My friend, it is not a problem that you do not have the same gifts as another. Be grateful for what you have. After all, it is not your wish – is it? – to be a medium in the way that others are. Your task is healing. This is your central motive. Be true to that, and do not worry about that which you do not have. What you need will be given to you.

No Bob, you are not losing touch. Rather, things are settling down more.

Bob, if you ask what more you can be doing, the answer is clear to you and me. Create those moments of peace and quiet in which you can learn to be receptive to your contact with Spirit. Practice makes perfect, does it not? It is the practice of these quiet moments that will bear fruit for you. This is what I would recommend for you, my friend.

On New Year's Eve 2005–2006, with Joshua

Shalom, my friend. Yes, I have indeed teaching to give you this evening.

It is a great joy for me that you once again make conscious contact with me and so enable me to communicate through and with you.

Yes, my friend, we do indeed stand on the threshold between past and future, between the old and the new, between what 'was' and what will 'become'. The truth of this needs to be brought home to many people at this time.

My friend, much will change and is already doing so. But above all else there is a great change in consciousness and awareness. People are waking up to the Spirit, albeit often in a confused and unclear way, but waking up nonetheless. The world of matter and sense is no longer able to satisfy many human souls. The search for meaning is on, and this search cannot rest with matter and material things. The world is in a state of flux. Changes are occurring at all levels.

Yes, even the seeming natural disasters and catastrophes that sweep over the planet are nothing else but a symptom of these important changes. We know only too well what abject misery and suffering many of these changes entail. And yet this must be, because human beings do not willingly suffer change. Instead they cling on to their old ways of living and of thinking. And these ways are geared to material comfort and well-being. We suffer with you, we feel your pain, but we also know that these sufferings and pains are but the birth pangs of the new age – the age that must supersede this present time.

You, my friend, suffer also with all that takes place in the world. You care for it and are shaken by these things. But rest assured that all will be well. Yes, this is not a mere platitude or trite saying. We say it because it is written in the stars – in the web of world destiny. All will be well because He who sacrificed Himself for mankind is with you. He will never leave you alone. His power, His love, will overcome all obstacles, all resistance to change and stagnation. The God of love is indissolubly linked to your world and He will help all those who come to Him. This should be known, not merely believed. Knowledge of the Spirit is needed, my son, in order to overcome the superstitions and theories of science, religion, and philosophy and other branches of so-called knowledge. The God of love and light has indeed united Himself with all mankind. Yes it is time, my friend, for mankind to awaken, to open their eyes and see the reality of the world; a reality which is much more than flesh and blood, matter and solid ground beneath your feet. Yes it is time to build a new ground beneath your feet; a new ground formed from love of the Spirit. This ground will not disappear, will not fail, will not crumble away. This ground is as firm as a rock – the rock of truth. This ground must be formed through the conviction of men's hearts and souls.

This, my friend, is what I wanted to say to you this New Year's Eve. This is the teaching I give unto you and with it I send my blessings and love and peace.

Shalom, my friend. God's Peace be with you now and for ever more. Yours, Joshua Isaiah.

Is it all right to share this teaching with others?

Shalom, my friend. You ask if it is all right to share this teaching with others. My answer is as follows:

Share it if you can, if others are willing to listen to it. But never attempt to impose it on those who are unwilling to receive it in the right spirit. It will merely fall on deaf ears. For those who are ready, it will be a help and strength to their souls. For others the time is not yet. So, my friend, use your discretion. Do what you feel is best. This is my advice to you, my friend. I wish you well and may all blessings be on your work and tasks. God be with you. Shalom, my friend. Oh, and a Happy New Year!

13 January 2006

Shalom, my friend. Thank you for contacting me once again and for giving me the opportunity to communicate through you. Yes, I do indeed have teaching to give you this evening, my friend.

It concerns the path of inner development, a path you have been walking along for many years. This is not an easy path to follow and yet, in our time, it is very necessary that more and more people turn to the life of the Spirit. This can be done, of course, in many ways. There are many ways or paths to scale the mountain peak.

The path you have chosen is one that leads through thinking to the peak, to the Spirit. Other paths suit other people. Each must find what is right and true for them – according to need and possibility. But my friend, you also have mediumistic abilities which you are using now in receiving my words and committing them to paper. These words flow into your mind almost effortlessly. Is it not so?

This is a wonderful ability, my friend, and I urge you to use it to the full. Many people would like to be able to do what you are doing now. You can do this because you have prepared yourself for this over many lifetimes. This is not simply the result of one single life in striving for the Spirit. You are given a unique, special opportunity to bring Spirit down on to paper. This we would urge you to use to the full; not simply for your own benefit but for the benefit of your fellows.

Your ability to write clearly is a gift, my friend, which it would be wise or good for you to practise further. Another book in which the reality of Spirit or, if you like, the working of Spirit is conveyed to others would be a worthy endeavour, would it not? Think on this, my friend.

See what comes to pass; what opportunities come your way. Your healing path progresses well; we know that this is close to your heart, and rest assured you are being guided and helped along this healing path. Only trust, my friend. Learn to trust and have faith. Faith can move mountains! Even the mountain in your own heart! Allow the Spirit to flow through you; move yourself out of the way and good things will come to pass through you.

This is the teaching I wished to give you this evening. Receive it with our blessing and love. We watch over you from Spirit and endeavour to guide you and help in every way that we can. Shalom, my friend. Peace be with you. Peace of heart and peace of mind. Joshua.

Although Joshua is giving teaching about my particular path of inner development, it may well be that others who also walk their own inner path can gain help in some way, or encouragement, from what is written here – for example, learning to trust in the Spirit and oneself. I very much hope so.

26 January 2006

Shalom, my friend. Thank you for getting into contact with me once again. Yes, there is teaching that I wish to give you this evening. Once again the teaching concerns your path of inner development.

My friend, you are making much progress even though this may not be apparent to you. It is often the case that progress is made but is not evident to the one whom it concerns. The progress which you are making is to do with trusting in the Spirit, which you rightly see as your main lesson in this incarnation.

Trusting in the Spirit is an affair of the heart, not of the head!

However much you may think, however much you may know with your head, trusting in the Spirit cannot be learnt from books. It has to be learnt through life itself. This, my friend, you are learning and this is good. Well done, my friend, for this lesson is the most important in your life.

If you look back to your childhood, you will clearly see how you needed to find trust in life. This trust was not strong in you. You doubted yourself. You lacked self-confidence. You were anxious and afraid in many ways, and this at root was, and is, a matter of trust. Trust, trust, trust, my friend. Trust in God always and walk in the footsteps of the Master, the Lord Jesus. This is the teaching I wished to give you this evening, my friend.

Thank you once again for allowing me to transmit my words through you in clear consciousness and awareness. You have become, you see, a very able instrument for the Spirit to express itself through.

Communicating with Joshua (II)

Shalom, my friend. God's blessings be upon you and peace be with you. Shalom for now until we speak again, though know, of course, that I am always with you and, so to speak, by your side.

Your teacher and friend in Spirit. Joshua Isaiah.

Let us once again give ourselves a short, hygienic break in these teachings, because there is still more to come in the next chapter.

Communicating with Joshua (III)

I believe that each of us has guides and helpers in Spirit. We are, in reality, never left alone to just fend for ourselves. It seems that way sometimes, of course, because we do not turn our so busy thoughts and minds to the friends who patiently stand by us invisibly. However, the moment we begin to think of them and take them into consideration, we begin to open the door of our hearts to allow them into our ordinary lives, consciously. When the links are thus formed, knowledge and certainty and communication can grow, and also gratitude! As my medium friend, Anne, pointed out, 'the dead are but a thought away.' And that, I reckon, is pretty close!

12 February 2006

Shalom, my friend. I am grateful that you once again make contact with me. Yes, my friend, I have another teaching for you this evening. It concerns, my friend, your way of life.

You have at present an interest in many things. Your mind is very active and your interest is aroused to learn many new things. This is all to the good, my friend. It belongs to your natural enthusiasm. However, take care, my friend, that you do not overdo things. Moderation in all things is the key to success.

Persevere in your interests, my friend, as they will indeed bear fruit. Yes I know that you see these activities as a part of your path of development and training. So be it. Yes they can indeed help you along life's way. However, take time – Rome wasn't built in a day – and neither can you achieve your goals in haste. Patience, my friend, is needed. This is not always your greatest strength!

You ask why you are getting strong bodily sensations, movements [when communicating telepathically], it is because I am very close to you and my energy is enmeshed with yours. This is what brings about your bodily movements. It is nothing to worry about, my friend. So my lesson to you is to 'take care' and 'proceed slowly' and with due consideration but, on the other hand, persevere towards your aims and take all things as a learning experience.

This is what I wanted to say to you this evening. Teaching for your own good and personal benefit.

Shalom, my friend. All blessings be with you. Your teacher and friend in Spirit. Joshua Isaiah.

19 February 2006 (on Scilly)

Shalom, my friend. Yes you are right when you say that you have not established regular times for sitting in the silence. However, this does not matter, in the sense that it is not essential for communication between us. The link is formed and you can communicate with me at will, as you are doing now. However, this is not to say, my friend, that you would not gain immeasurably by learning to sit in the silence regularly. It would help you to gain that peace of mind for which you long, and which seems to you so elusive. So let me, my friend, encourage you once again to try to enter into the silence on a regular basis. It will bring you good fruits.

Yes, my friend, I do have a lesson to give you this evening. It concerns the value and meaning of life. My friend, you have already made progress on the inner path – you have searched for meaning and purpose for a long time. You know that the true meaning and value of life is not to be found in the acquisition of outer things, of material gain and comfort. Continue to search for truth, my friend. Do not diminish your efforts to seek the truth in life. Yes you may say that one man's truth is another man's 'poison' – for want of a better word. However, truth is truth. Truth is not merely subjective and personal, it is objective and general. It is for this truth in life that you should continue to seek. Remember, my friend, the words of the master, Jesus: 'I am the way and the truth and the life.' To seek the truth is to seek the master – the Christ within. Yes, you ask, 'How can I find the truth within? How shall I go about it?' Seek knowledge, my friend, true self-knowledge. To seek such self-knowledge is not easy; it is not plain sailing, so to speak. It entails discomfort, nay sometimes suffering and hardships, but it is the only way to find the truth of oneself – who one really is behind the illusion of matter. Therefore, my friend, I encourage you – adjure you – to seek such knowledge, such understanding, such enlightenment. In doing so, you will find the truth and, as the Bible says, 'The truth will set you free.' To be free we must know ourselves.

Bob, this is the teaching I wished to give you this evening. If you wish to ask me questions feel free to do so, my friend.

Why are my thoughts so problematic? Why do I still experience negative, disquieting, things mentally?

My friend, I have told you before that these things are a test; a test of your own striving and betterment. Replace these disquieting thoughts with the thoughts you want to have! Consciously put other thoughts and images in place of those you dislike. You see, my friend, it is the conscious control and direction of your thoughts that is called for. Take your experiences as an opportunity that is given you to improve matters, to

> gain greater freedom and control. Don't dwell on the negative. You know this does not help at all. Turn away from the negative and replace it with the positive. In this way you will, in time, achieve what you wish for, namely, peace of mind.
>
> Yes, my friend, you are right. Distractions abound and there are forces that draw one away from one's spiritual practices. However, my friend, do not despair. Remember that each day gives new opportunities and new chances to do what you didn't do yesterday!
>
> Shalom, my friend. Your interest in judo is interesting. It is, after all, a form of self-discipline. I wish you luck with it. But progress slowly. Take care and do not rush forward. If you wish to do it, why not? You are fit enough for it. But proceed slowly and act wisely!
>
> Shalom, my friend. Thank you for again making contact with me. God's greetings and blessings, my friend. Yours, Joshua.

Is it not impressive with what patience and understanding Joshua deals with my oft-repeated queries about disturbing thoughts? I believe we all have guides who have tolerance, kindness, and forbearance with us, in spite of our own impatience and, sometimes, negative self-criticisms.

23 February 2006

Do you have any further teachings/lessons to give me at this time?

> Shalom, my friend. Yes I do have another lesson to give you tonight. It is this.
>
> You often wonder about the meaning of your life. Not so? The direction and task that you should move in. Well let me say this, my friend. At present you are doing all that you can where you are. Changes will

come, yes, but the timing of change is all important.
Trust, my friend, that you will be shown when a
change is needed.

Remember, my friend, that there is guidance in life.
Yes, guidance, not only from guides but also from your
own soul. You yourself have made the plan. You
yourself know, deep within, what lies in store. Of
course, you cannot be shown all that – you must be
free to choose – but you will choose according to your
destiny, your star. So, my friend, this is the lesson.
Trust in destiny. Trust in your plan, hidden though it
may be as yet.

Life will show you the way. Do not worry. Have
trust and faith. There is a greater wisdom behind your
life, your own soul's wisdom.

Shalom, my friend. This is what I wanted to tell you
this night. God bless. Shalom, shalom, shalom. Joshua.

With this teaching, I feel there is much to learn for all of us. How often we worry ourselves sick not knowing which way to turn or what direction to go in. We have a star to follow; we must only look up to it, instead of having our nose to the ground and only seeing that which is in front of our eyes at that moment in time. We are so often blind and deaf to our own destiny, our own plan!

Now I turn to the communications in my last notebook, the fifth, to share with you, my reader.

27 February 2006

Could the teachings you give me from Spirit also be important for others to know about?

Shalom, my friend. Yes indeed, the teachings I can give
to you can also be important and valuable for others to
hear about and receive. You have, my friend, the ability
to bring through these teachings, to receive and

transmit them. This is a gift, my friend, which you would do well to use. Yes, not simply for your own sake, but for the benefit of others. My friend, this is the answer to your question.

Have you a teaching to give me right now, this morning, or not?

My friend, I do have a teaching to give you. Please receive it in good spirit. The teaching concerns your conduct of life. You must, my friend, strive harder to acquire knowledge – knowledge of yourself. This is, as you know, the basis of all true knowledge. Not for nothing were the halls of wisdom given the words: 'Oh man, know thyself.'

In these words you find indeed the meaning and purpose of life. Self-knowledge, my friend, is what you should strive to attain. This self-knowledge can only be won through hardships and difficulties. This is the challenge of life itself. Such self-knowledge is not given easily. It is not an easy route. It requires, my friend, much effort and persistence. This is what I wanted to impress upon you today, now. Take heart, my friend, you have already made good steps along this way. But I urge you to continue, to seek, to find, to struggle onwards, so that through this struggle you may help your fellow men. This, my friend, is the purpose, the aim, the task, of self-knowledge: to help others.

Bob, you are already doing this more than you yourself realise. It is my hope and wish that you will continue to grow in spirit and soul. You will, my friend, if you persevere. To give and not receive should be your goal. Then you yourself will indeed receive what you need also.

This is the teaching I wished to give you. Shalom, my friend. Persevere on your path of knowledge. It is the man of knowledge who attains freedom. The truth will make you free.

Shalom, my friend. Peace be with you, and thank you for making this contact today. Yours, Joshua.

This teaching on the importance of self-knowledge in our search for meaning and purpose in our lives is clearly applicable to everyone. Without self-knowledge we do not really attain knowledge of the world, and without this we continue to walk in darkness and ignorance. There are many paths, each must choose his or her way, but each must lead to the same goal: 'Oh man, know thyself!'

2 March 2006

Shalom, my friend. Yes it is possible for me to draw near to you at this time, because I am never far away.

Joshua, you say I am making progress on the inner path of self-development and knowledge, and yet I don't feel that I am getting very far. Please explain!

My friend, I understand your feelings. It is not easy to know about one's inner progress. The person concerned is not always the best judge of this.

However, be assured, my friend, that whether or not you feel it or realise it, you are nonetheless making progress, even good progress I would say. The main thing, my friend, is to strive for truth. Seek the truth and the rest will follow. Truth and knowledge belong together. And so does love. Love, truth and knowledge should be your goals, my friend. On this pathway much progress can be made, but it takes time and patience. No haste, less speed, but steadily plodding on. This is the best advice I can give. Other powers will grant you the gifts which you deserve, which you have earned, so to speak.

So, my friend, do not worry. Worry helps not at all. Rather have confidence and trust in your way, your path of life. As you know, nothing is without meaning and purpose and value – even the difficult experiences. Each according to his measure – this is the rule. So, Bob, in answer to your question, I can tell you that you are indeed making progress inwardly, even though this does not feel so to you.

The most important progress has to do with trust. Trust in the guidance given you and all will be well.

Your friend and guide, Joshua.

And now a short teaching on a lighter note with regard to one of my latest interests and pursuits!

3 March 2006

Is it permissible to ask for inspiration and help in judo from its original founder and master, Jigoro Kano, who died in 1938?

Shalom, my friend. You pose an interesting question, which I cannot say I have had before. You ask if it is justified or justifiable to turn to the founder of judo in order to seek from him inspiration and help in your learning of this art.

Well, my friend, my answer is yes: you may indeed turn to the spirit being of the founder of judo because he carries a responsibility for bringing this art and impulse into the world. You may indeed, in the right spirit, ask him for help and guidance. There is nothing wrong in this, provided you do not misuse any help you are given.

Other people turn in thought to the founders of their religions, so why should you not turn to the founder of judo if that is your wish and desire? Only take care that your motives are pure and of good intent. That is the safeguard.

> It will be interesting to see if you can receive the inspiration and help that you seek. Why not? Seek and you will find. This is the law.
>
> So I wish you luck, my friend, in your endeavour and in your sport. Greetings and blessings, my friend. Shalom, shalom, shalom. Joshua.

Well, dear reader, to satisfy your curiosity, I have not yet tried to make this link with Jigoro Kano – but I still might! Just imagine, if you also have a particular sport or other burning interest, who might be there on the other side itching to help you along if you would but ask!

9 March 2006

> Shalom, my friend. Yes you may, of course, ask me some questions if you wish to. After all I am, as you say, your guide and teacher in Spirit. So please fire away, so to speak.

Joshua, I was just holding some quartz crystals and had a very strong reaction which went through my whole body. Why was this?

> My friend, you know the answer to your question already. The energies flowing through the crystals react strongly with your own energy field. This is due to the sensitivity which you have towards the energies. Thus you get such a strong and definite reaction. As you know this is nothing to worry about; it is for you quite natural actually.

Do the crystal energies help me in any way?

> Yes, my friend, the energies from your crystals can strengthen your own energy field. The crystals act as transmitters and channel powerful energies into your

own aura which can be used in a beneficial way. You know that you could, if you wished, develop your own abilities to use crystals in your healing work. However, this choice is left entirely up to you. I can only tell you that you have a propensity for using these crystal energies if you so wish.

S, my friend, is coming to see me today for conversation and healing. Do you have any message, teaching for her, or me, or both of us?

Shalom, my friend. Yes I have teaching that both of you can benefit from. S is also very sensitive, as you are, and for this reason also vulnerable and exposed to influences that can be harmful. She needs to take care to protect herself sufficiently, as you should also, my friend. There are forces for good and also forces for evil. You should therefore take care to admit only that which is helpful and good, and shun that which is harmful in any way.

How can we protect ourselves?

My friend, you can both protect yourselves by putting a wall of armour around you. I mean, of course, armour of light and love. Such armour cannot be penetrated by the powers of darkness. This invisible armour can protect you at all times. It is invincible.

Yes, but how does one fashion and create such armour?

By all your good thoughts and deeds. Good thoughts are realities in Spirit, much more real than people ordinarily imagine. People, in fact, have no idea how powerful their thoughts are. At least the thoughts they could have if they learnt to focus them strongly. The power of good thoughts creates the armour to protect you.

Do not doubt for one moment the reality of these things. They are indeed realities as real as anything you call real in the world of sense. This, my friend, is a teaching that would benefit both your friend and yourself, because you are both sensitive in your own right.

Joshua, you know that even now I harbour some doubts as to the objectivity, rather than subjectivity, of the thought messages I receive. Are you disappointed about this?'

No, Bob, I am not disappointed. It is only natural to doubt and, for you, this is doubly so! You doubt because you want certainty of knowledge. Well, my friend, let the truth – the reality – of what comes through you speak for itself. What does it matter, my friend, what source these thoughts come from if they contain truth? The truth will speak for itself. So let this be your guide, my friend. Let the truth speak to you. Then it matters not whether you believe the thoughts are given you from me or whether you imagine them to come from yourself in some fashion. What is true cannot be denied. What is untrue should be rejected and discounted. This, my friend, is how I would advise you to proceed.

Whether you believe it or not, I am still there with you and will continue to help and guide and teach you as far as I am able. Shalom, my friend. All blessings on your work and life. Your friend in Spirit, Joshua.

Joshua, could I learn to see you as my medium friend Anne can do? I feel this would help me 'believe' in your presence more strongly. Is this possible for me?

My friend, if you wanted to have an image of me, to see me, so to speak, you could do so. It is not as difficult as you imagine. Simply create a screen in your mind and let it remain clear. Then I can project my image on to your mind-screen. Try it, my friend, and see what you get. You may be surprised by how easily this can come to you.

Shalom, my friend. Take care.

Before the following communication with Joshua, I had been in telepathic contact with my mother and father who made their transitions about five and eleven years ago respectively. 11 March was my mother's earthly birthday.

11 March 2006

Shalom, my friend. Yes your mother was right; I also want to speak with you this evening. Shalom, my friend. Peace be with you.

My friend, you are making great progress in receiving us from Spirit in spite of your doubts. You see your constitution is such that you are an excellent receiving station, so to speak. The thoughts flow into you effortlessly and this, of course, is the very reason why you doubt their authenticity! This is understandable, but nonetheless it is a reality that you are receiving correctly the thoughts from Spirit. You see, my friend, you have always lived strongly in your thinking. That's why you have so many problems! Problems arise through thinking and the many questions and doubts that it raises. So it is. However, we call upon you, my friend, to trust the messages you receive. They can be of value not only for you but also for others. Already you have some notion of this from your friend S. Not so? She has been led to you by destiny and karma. You sense this, both of you, and you will see in time where this will lead. It may surprise you both. Now I have some teaching to give you, my friend, and it is this.

You come to earth to fulfil your destiny and karma. This is the meaning and value of earth existence. We know this is not easy. We know the problems involved.

We know the trials and obstacles that are placed in your paths. But we know also that the meaning of life can only be fulfilled when you say 'yes' to your karma and destiny. To go with the flow, this is important. To fight against your destiny is to fight against yourself. And to fight against yourself brings grief and sorrow. Destiny is there for you to fulfil. It is the path you yourselves have chosen. Therefore, to fight against this is to fight against yourself.

Accept that what will be, will be. Learn to accept that which happens in your life. Accept it with gratitude. Accept it even if it is very hard to stomach. Yes, your friend S could benefit from this teaching. Her life has been very hard. She has had great problems to overcome and to accept. She does not accept much that has happened to her. And yet she herself fashioned her own destiny. Tell her this, my friend; it will help her. She fights against it. She rebels, so to speak, and has great anger. This must change if she is to move on. You can help her to do this – to lift this great burden from her heart.

So this is the teaching I give you tonight, my friend. The teaching to accept and be grateful for your destiny, however hard and unjust it may appear. It is your destiny, your karma, your choice and decision. You have created it. You must live it. You can change it for the better, but work with it not against it.

Shalom, my friend. God's greeting be with you and to your friend. All blessings. Your guide and teacher in Spirit, Joshua Isaiah.

Joshua, can I contact and converse with others that I have known, in Spirit, if I so wish?

Shalom, my friend. Yes you can indeed converse with others if you so wish and if they also wish to contact and converse with you, which, in all likelihood, they would wish to do.

Communicating with Joshua (III)

We long on this side of life to find those who will receive our thoughts and messages. You cannot imagine how difficult this is – how sorrowful – when we want to speak to you and no one listens. We long to share with you the wonders and blessings from our side of the river, so to speak, but there are few indeed who have the ears to hear. This causes much suffering to us. There is so much that could be said; so much to share with you all. So, my friend, do make yourself available for those who wish to communicate through you. They will indeed take the opportunity you give them and be full of gratitude for the opportunity. You have no idea how much this would mean for them. Think of this further, my friend, and do what you feel is right and proper.

Your friend in Spirit, Joshua Isaiah.

Would Rudolf Steiner, the founder of anthroposophy, approve of this way of communication?

Yes, my friend, he would approve wholeheartedly. You do what you do in full consciousness. You are neither in trance, nor hypnotised, nor in any other sense subdued. What more can you ask for? You have the gift of clairaudience, of receiving telepathically the thoughts of others. This surely your friend and teacher Rudolf Steiner would approve of. So let your mind and heart be at peace. Proceed slowly, towards the goal. All will then be well. This is enough for tonight, my friend.

Shalom. Peace be with you. Joshua.

I wrote to Anne, the spiritual medium, and sent her a copy of one of Joshua's lessons, and asked her if she could check with him if this had really come from him! In other words, I sought confirmation of the truth of my own capacity to receive aright. Anne asked Joshua for his input on what I had asked in my letter and he confirmed, through her, that he was communicating with me. I was very moved by the tone of Anne's ninth reading for me, and I myself contacted Joshua again directly.

13 March 2006

> Shalom, my friend. Thank you for contacting me once again so soon. I am glad that you are happy with the message you have received from your friend Anne. Yes she is a good friend and helper, Bob. I hope this message serves to convince you of my presence, my friend. I am truly here with you. Yes it is, because this ability is so natural to you that you even doubt its very reality. However, my friend, doubt not. Know the truth. The truth that I am communicating through you. For this I am eternally grateful, my friend. You do not even now realise what a blessing it is to find an able communicator like yourself. My friend, you have a great gift which I hope you will develop and use to the full. Not only for your own sake, but for the sake of others. So many people would long to be able to do what you can do so effortlessly; namely, to receive thoughts from Spirit. Treasure this gift, my friend, and use it wisely. If you use it in the right way it will bring blessings and help to those in need.
>
> Yes, my friend, there is something else I wish to say to you. It is: have faith in yourself, have faith in your own abilities, strive to always do what is good and true. This will give you the protection that you need. It is like the armour I described to you recently. So, Bob, continue to do what you know to be good and true and no harm can befall you. I send you now my love and greetings and send also my grateful thoughts for all that you are doing. Yours, Joshua.

To have faith in oneself – in one's best and true self – is this not a challenge for many of us?

Life in Spirit

I had had the thought on the morning of 14 March 2006 of asking Joshua about life in the spirit world. I felt that to receive communications about this could be of great interest, value, and benefit to others who wonder what the afterlife is like. This was a question I put to Joshua to see what he thought about this idea; to see if he would be positive that we would take this up as a theme for some time.

> Shalom, my friend. Yes the theme you suggest is interesting and important. I, for my part, am quite willing to communicate with you on this subject and, as you say, it could prove of great benefit for others who wish to know about life in Spirit. So yes, Bob, let us cooperate in this way and see where it leads us.
> Your friend and teacher in Spirit, Joshua.

Time was not wasted to begin this theme, as well as continuing with other questions and answers.

Life in Spirit (I)

> Shalom, my friend. We meet again. This is becoming a habit! A good one I may add. Yes, the subject of 'life in Spirit'; where shall we start my friend?
> Well, let us begin where we are now, shall we? You are in the body; I am in the light of Spirit. Here we have a beginning, you see. In Spirit we are bathed in light; surrounded by light; filled with light; living light; breathing light; eating light. Light is everywhere. Our

bodies are light. Our thoughts are light. Everything is light and nowhere is darkness – not in Spirit. You see, my friend, that light is the substance of the universe. Yes, of course, love also. Light and love belong together. But here, for a moment, I concentrate on the light. It is said that the light shines in the darkness and this is true, my friend. You live in darkness – darkness and weight. We live in light and levity. There is no weight here in Spirit, no gravity, no pull downwards. No, we rise ever upward on our forward path of evolution and development. We move from sphere to sphere, from level to level. We move along life's pathway towards the heights of heaven. Can you understand this, my friend? Can you begin to imagine how glorious this is? It is not easy to describe in earthly thoughts or words. It is majestic to behold and we are filled with gratitude that we are allowed to behold what we do. You wonder: what do you do?

Well, my friend, we weave in the light, we play in the light, we strive for the light – the greater light, the higher light, the true light of Spirit. All beings here live in the light. They are the light. We are truly beings of light, Bob. You cannot imagine this easily I think, not when you are dressed – clothed – in matter. The freedom of light, the freedom of thought, the light of worlds – in this we live and breathe and have our being.

This is the beginning of the journey into Spirit, Bob – the start of our exploration of life in Spirit. It is perhaps enough as a beginning. We will speak more of this; will explore together regions and domains and spheres of spirit life in order to answer the questions you have.

Yes, there will be many questions. We will look at them, answer them if we can, and so try to do what we have set ourselves as a task. For now, my friend, shalom, shalom, shalom. Peace be with you and God's blessing. Yours Joshua.

16 March 2006

Why should anyone want to leave this light-filled spirit life to be incarnate again? Whose will is it?

> Shalom, my friend. You ask about reincarnation and karma. This is important; interesting. Yes, why indeed, your friend asks, should we leave the realm of light and love to incarnate again on earth? The answer to this question you know, of course, already.
>
> You cannot develop further if you remain in the light of Spirit only. Only on earth can you meet and fulfil your own individual destiny and karma. This is why you must incarnate. You have tasks to do on earth which cannot be done elsewhere. You must transform both yourselves and the earth. The earth must become a planet of love. You cannot perform this by staying in heaven. The immensity of the task cannot be denied. But this is the reason why you come to earth. Not even the angels can do this in heaven. They look with awe and wonder to see what human beings can do. They give their love and blessings to your efforts, but they themselves cannot do it. Only you who live in the body can bring about this transformation. This, my friend, is the answer to your question.

Life in Spirit (II)

> Shalom, my friend. We meet once again. You see how easy it is for you to contact me and for communication to take place. This should hearten you, my friend, and give you greater confidence in your abilities. Well done!
>
> Now to your further question, or questions, about life in Spirit. What do we do here, how do we live, and what does it look like?
>
> Well let us begin with what we do. We live in the

Life in Spirit

light, we weave in the light, we serve and create the light by our being and our attitudes. Light is a reality, my friend. It is a substance and material you could say, with which we build bridges, houses, cars (cars?). Yes you hear me aright, strange though it sounds. We construct out of light what we need; we fashion the light; we mould the light as you mould wood and stone on earth. Yes you find it strange that I say 'cars'. How can it be, you ask, that cars can exist in the Spirit? Well they can, but not like cars on earth. We have also to travel from place to place, from sphere to sphere. How can we do this? We build cars of light, vehicles of light, vessels of light in which we can sit and move. Yes, you are getting this aright. I am testing you, my friend, to see if you will faithfully put down my thoughts and not yours, even when you find these thoughts incredulous and unbelievable! It is a test, my friend, in communication.

Of course we do not have cars like the cars on earth, this would be ludicrous indeed. But still we have means of travelling from sphere to sphere and, for this, I have used the word 'car'. After all, what is a car in reality? Nothing else but a vessel, a vehicle, a means of travelling. It is in this sense that I use the word. Well done for putting it down as I said it, even though you couldn't believe it! It was, as I say, a test. Do not take it amiss.

So, as I say, we build from light. We use this substance to create what we need. It is available everywhere here and we can learn to control it for our purposes and intentions. You find this strange? You wonder: do I hear aright? Am I spinning out fantasies, you ask yourself? Well, life in Spirit is strange to you on earth. It is different; it is new to your thoughts and ideas and to communicate any of this to you I must use words that you know. Without this, no communication is possible. This is why you will find some ideas strange and unbelievable.

Let me tell you more about life on this side. We eat and drink as you do, but not, of course, earthly substances. We drink the light of Spirit, we fill ourselves with God's will, and we do that which serves the good to the best of our abilities. This is our work; this is our task. Of course, as on earth, some can do more, others less. We are not all the same. Each according to his measure. Our abilities vary, our capacities differ and yet, my friend, we work together to serve the good, which is God. There are in fact many tasks. Your friend John is engaged in healing work with you and others; I in teaching and guiding. Your mother and father are coming into their own field of work in helping and guiding others also. All our work is related and connected. We do not work for ourselves, but for others. We do not get paid in any earthly sense, but in a very real sense we are paid in kind. What goes out comes back. Is this not so, my friend? Worlds are born in our work; stars are made to shine and glow and become. Does all this sound too fantastic to you? Well, Bob, I speak truly of what I see and know. It is my task to teach and it is teaching which you have requested. So bear with me, my friend. Keep an open mind. Do not dismiss lightly that which seems to you strange and improbable. This is itself a test for you in open-mindedness and receptivity. Do not judge by earthly standards. Remember you are learning about heavenly, spiritual things. I think you have received as much as you can for today. You must also exercise hygiene in your communication with me, lest you fall into the temptation of talking with me all the time! I mean this humorously, my friend. But it is still good to know when to stop, as in any conversation. So for tonight, my friend, I wish you God's greetings and blessings. We shall talk again soon. Your friend and teacher, Joshua.

19 March 2006 (a few days later)

Will I be allowed to see auras and chakras that can help me in my healing work? Would it not be a great advantage to see something of the energy field, the subtle bodies, and energy centres?

> Shalom, my friend. Yes, your question is both interesting and understandable. I can quite well appreciate that you would like to be able to see auras and chakras and energy fields, in order to assist you in your healing work. However, my friend, your healing does not depend on these things. The healing which you give is beneficial to people, even though you cannot see exactly how the energies are working and responding. You believe it would help you in your healing work if you could see these things, but actually this is quite unnecessary. As you know, Bob, you are but the instrument for healing and those who direct the healing know already what they are doing. They know exactly where the energies are needed and required. Yes, my friend, it would give you some satisfaction to actually see these energies and the effect they have on those to whom you give healing but, I repeat, it is not necessary for you to see these things.
>
> Now, whether or not you will be allowed, so to speak, to see auras and energies is not for me to say. I do not know. This will depend on others. If this is something you earnestly wish for then I suggest, my friend, that you ask for it. If you ask then you may also receive. If you do not ask then surely it cannot be that important for you. So this is my answer to your question this morning – ask for what you wish/want and wait and see if the answer is forthcoming. Perhaps you will be surprised.

Will I be allowed, enabled, permitted to see you, as Anne my medium friend is able to see you?

> Shalom, my friend. You wish to see me, then why not? Already we are bound together through our communication. I merge with you when you are writing and receiving my thoughts. So if you wish to see me, why not ask? You have not asked until now to see me. Not true? You have been content to receive the thought messages, as you do now. So, my friend, again my advice to you is to ask. Ask and you receive – this is the law of Spirit. It is the law that the Master taught to his disciples. It is the law that still holds good today. But when you ask, mean it, Bob. Ask not just out of curiosity, but out of earnestness and intent. The asking must be sincere and true, and then the Spirit will respond accordingly.
> See how you fare, Bob. Ask and see what is given to you. Does not your Father in heaven know what you need even before you ask? Indeed He does. But it is still up to you to ask. In this you have your freedom.
> Shalom, my friend. It was good to speak with you once more. Shalom, shalom, shalom. Peace be with you. Joshua.

Four days later, I had the idea of writing a book (this book) containing our communications, and also those with Dr John and my parents. So I decided to ask Joshua what he thought about this.

21 March 2006

> Shalom, my friend. Yes the idea of writing a book is certainly interesting and worthwhile. Give it thought, Bob. Do not rush into things on impulse. Consideration is due; but having considered all aspects, do what you feel to be right. I leave this up to you, my friend. It is your choice.

Yes, I have indeed pointed out the great need felt by those on this side of life to find those with whom they can communicate on earth. This need is there. To make others aware of this would also be a worthy task, a fitting task. But know, Bob, that your words may be met by ridicule and scorn. Be prepared for this. Not everyone will take kindly to such a book. There is a certain risk involved. However, life itself is a risk, is it not?

I do not wish to put you off this task, Bob. It is, after all, a task which needs to be done. To share what you know – to bring this to a wider audience – yes this would be good. So see how you feel about it; ask others who are sympathetic to this and, from all this, make up your own mind. I will help you as much as I am able to, but the responsibility must be yours. You understand this, Bob, I know that. However, I say all this just to make you aware of the complexity of the task. There will certainly be those who cannot take you seriously. There will be others who will applaud your efforts. So these are my thoughts. Consider them and feel free to proceed as you will. You have my support either way. Peace be with you. Shalom, shalom, shalom. Joshua.

Life in Spirit (III)

23 March 2006

Is it better for you if I ask specific questions or if I simply receive what you wish/are able to convey?

> Shalom, my friend. It is good to be with you once again. With regard to your question as to whether it is better/easier for you to ask questions about life in Spirit, or to leave me quite free to convey to you what I can, I have no hard and fast feelings about this. I leave it up to

Life in Spirit

you, my friend, to proceed as you wish. If you choose to ask me specific questions then I will endeavour to answer them. If, however, you prefer simply to receive what I can give you on any one occasion, so be it. Either way I am more than happy to work with you on this theme.

You ask what it is like in Spirit? Well I will tell you, my friend.

It is full of joy and blessing that we are allowed to work as we do. Yes we also receive higher guidance – we are not left alone; we are helped at every stage – but we are also free to use our own initiative in a creative process. Can you understand this, my friend? On the one hand we feel supported and guided and helped and, on the other hand, we must take responsibility for what we do. As you know, my role is as a teacher. This is my chosen task. I do it willingly and with joy. I teach many others, Bob, not only you. There is much to learn and much to convey and therefore many of us are involved in this teaching task.

Even as on earth you have universities and schools, so here on the higher planes we also have our places of learning and instruction and education. Does this seem strange to you. Too much like home ground? Well, Bob, I can only tell you how it is. We have much to convey to human souls; we have much to learn and teach to those who are open and willing to listen. It is, of course, a pain for us that so many souls remain deaf and blind to what we impart. They are not open, not ready, not developed enough to hear our words or to receive our images or thoughts. This is why it is such a blessing that you, and others like you, are ready to receive what we so willingly convey.

Life in Spirit. It is a sort of bliss. Yes, a heavenly bliss. What do I mean by bliss? What can this convey to you, my friend? It is a harmony: a harmonising, a working together for a common good, a common aim and purpose.

Yes, there is indeed purposefulness in what we do together. There is a plan. There is sense and direction and goals to be achieved. After all, you cannot surely imagine that things would be done aimlessly, without purpose or direction. This would indeed be chaotic and lead to yet further chaos. No, my friend, there is meaning and purpose.

Our teaching work is directed at enlightening souls, of helping them to be ready to make the great transition themselves. To know beforehand what one is coming to is a great help. It is a way of preparation, a way of being ready to receive and respond to that which will come to every soul that must leave the body and ascend to the heights.

So many, my friend, enter our realms unprepared: blind and deaf in soul and spirit. And this is difficult for them and us. It requires much work and patience to orientate these souls to the transition they have made. To make them aware that they no longer live in a body on earth, but have ascended into the light. Can you understand this, my friend? Can you understand how difficult this is for many who are rooted in matter and have given no thought to the Spirit?

You see, my friend, just to make the great transition does not automatically confer knowledge and understanding on those who have died. That knowledge and understanding must be won on earth, in the body, in the life between birth and death. This is why your earthly life is so indispensable, so valuable, so without precedent. It is the great school of life, in truth. Therefore no one day should be wasted or squandered. All experience is invaluable, is used, is needed as part of your learning and preparation.

Do convey this fact to others, my friend. Help them to realise the truth of what I am saying. It really is not for nothing that life presents such challenges to many of you. You yourselves have set these challenges before your own souls. You know in Spirit what is needed for your own soul's growth and maturity. Your destiny is your own – of your own making. Do not blame God for what goes wrong, for the hardships and the sufferings. You yourselves have set these tasks before you to live and learn by. Through suffering you grow and become; become strong in soul and spirit.

Believe me, my friend, when I tell you these things. They are the knowledge which you seek and which you can convey also to others if you choose to do so. As always, my friend, I leave these decisions up to you. You must make up your own mind. This is your freedom. My role is to teach, to give you knowledge, to answer your questions, to broaden your horizons, to expand your mind.

Is this perhaps enough for tonight? I could, of course, go on, but as I have mentioned before it is good not to attempt too much all at once. There is time enough to pick up the threads and continue our theme. If you are happy with this, my friend, we will stop and resume on another occasion. Good, so be it. Shalom, shalom, shalom, till we meet again. Joshua.

Life in Spirit (IV)

25 March 2006

Shalom, my friend. It is good to be with you once again. Yes, indeed, let us continue our theme of life in Spirit.

Life in Spirit is full of blessings. Our work is guided and helped in so many ways. We are not left alone to flounder so to speak, but are helped and supported and guided in the tasks we do. What do we do actually, you wonder? Well my friend, as I have said before, there are many tasks to be done here in Spirit. There is the task of healing the sick in mind and body, of bringing comfort and reassurance to those who are afraid and lost. There is the task of letting souls know that all is well with them, that their friends on earth are taken care of and watched over, so that they can put aside the fear and anger and emotions which can plague them and hinder them on their onward path. You see, my friend, there is much teaching and learning to do.

Those who pass over often do not know where they have arrived. They may not even realise that they have died. They are often confused and all at sea, so to speak. Therefore many of us here are engaged in educating and weaning these souls away from earthly ties and connections. This can take a long time, sometimes many earth years to achieve. However long it takes, it is a task that must be done for otherwise the soul remains earthbound and stuck in its ways. You see, my friend, so few people are prepared for what they meet here. They have not given a thought to spiritual things whilst alive on earth. To come here then is like being transplanted suddenly into a strange and bewildering land. Souls are lost and afraid, asleep to Spirit, still enmeshed in all the concerns of earthly life. You see, my friend, what a blessing it is that someone like you can so freely and easily receive thoughts from Spirit. Yes, these thoughts are the very substance of Spirit. Thoughts here are real, as real as the things you call real on earth, the things you can touch and feel. Solid matter does not exist here. There is no such thing as substantiality as you know it on the earth plane. No, light abounds, thoughts abound, beings abound, but not matter. Matter is an illusion of the senses. It is the veil in which you live in the body. There is a far greater reality and that is the reality in which we live here.

Again you wonder: 'What do you do?' Well, my friend, I have told you this already, did you not believe me perhaps? No, rather than not believe me you simply wonder what else people do in Spirit. Do they walk in gardens, do they talk to each other, do they go on holiday, do they have jobs, do they rise from sphere to sphere, do they marry and have children, do they do all those same sorts of things as they did on earth? No my friend, life in Spirit is very different from earthly life, so different that it is difficult to describe. It is not a light, higher version of earthly life. It is substantially different; quite unworldly, in fact. And yet there are some similarities; similarities in how people or souls relate to one another. You know, my friend, that the bond of love connects all souls. This is the bridge from soul to soul. Through love we draw close and in fact live in each other. Where there is no love, souls remain separate and isolated. Therefore, my friend, it is love which builds the bridge between all worlds – between heaven and earth. Love is the most important thing of all. Yes, St Paul attests to this. Without love there is barrenness and a desert land in which nothing grows or thrives. So, my friend, this is the teaching I wished to give you this evening. You will be surprised how many pages you have already written! But, you see, our contact flows easily and you are learning quickly to put down on paper the thoughts which flow from me into your mind. I am grateful for this, my friend. I am grateful for your trust and help. What would a teacher be without a good and able pupil? Well, not much, I can tell you.

So I send you all blessings and look forward in anticipation to the next time we shall meet and talk with each other. Yes, true, I am doing most of the talking! However, I do not think you mind this?

Shalom, shalom, shalom, my friend. Be at peace. Love and light. Joshua.

I have one more question still, Joshua. I am speaking now openly amongst friends and relatives about my contact with you, and John and mother. Is this all right, do you think, or should I rather remain silent about these things?

> Shalom, my friend. If you choose to speak openly about these things, it is all right with me. You, my friend, must be your own judge in these matters.
> There will be those who ridicule what you say because of their own disbelief, fear and scepticism. Others will take it gladly and be grateful for it. Bob, you must do what you feel is right. Is it not better to speak about what you know, than to keep this knowledge to yourself? Did not Jesus tell the disciples not to keep their light hidden under a bushel, but rather let it shine forth into the world? This takes some courage to do. But if the disciples did it, why not you? I believe this answers your question, my friend. Shalom, shalom, shalom.

28 March 2006

> Shalom, my friend. Yes, of course, you may ask me to draw near to you to communicate for a short time. In communication we become something of a oneness. I merge easily with you and this is why the communication is so easy and effortless. Yes, my friend, you wonder if this could happen at any time of the day. Yes it could, but only if you wish it so. This is part of your protection, my friend. You should invite me to draw near and then I can do so safely, so to speak. It is good to have clear limits on any form of communication. After all, my friend, you would not just wish anybody to slip in, so to speak, to enter the house uninvited.
> Yes, you are very sensitive to these things. This has

> to do with your particular constitution. Yes, it is the same reason why you react so easily and quickly to crystals. You pick up the vibrations like a sponge, so to speak. Therefore you do need also to be on your guard. It is always good practice to invite those with whom you wish to communicate; do not leave the door open for any intruders to walk in.

I was asked the other day if I could make contact with others on the other side if a request comes to me. What do you think?

> My friend, you could indeed make contact with others if they are willing and want to make contact through you. Indeed, you would be performing a service to others in this way. Only, as I said before, this should be done in the right way. After all, you do not want to become the pawn of any Tom, Dick or Harry, do you?
>
> You are very sensitive and open, my friend, to such contact. Our own communication proves just that. But as I said, care is needed and some discrimination.
>
> Always ask for God's protection when such contacts are made. Then only those who bear no ill will can gain entrance to your mind and thoughts. Your intentionality must be clear. Never do this selfishly or with other intentions, only as a service and blessing for others.
>
> Yes, my friend, there is something further I would say to you. Trust yourself, Bob. Have faith in yourself. Let your faith and trust grow so strong that nothing or nobody can shake it. This is what I wanted to say to you, my friend. For now, all blessings and love. Shalom, shalom, shalom. Joshua.

I had written to Anne my medium friend to ask her what she thought about the idea of my writing a book containing the communications, and also the contents of the readings she had done for me. Anne wrote back very positively about this idea. She wrote that, 'I personally would ask Joshua and Dr John to communicate a book to you of all they want sharing as readings and leave it to Spirit to provide the contents... Good luck with the writing, I have no doubts you and your team in Spirit can do it! Put me down for buying the first copy!'

I turned to Joshua to ask his views on this.

29 March 2006

> Shalom, my friend. Thank you for contacting me once again. Yes, with regard to the book that you want to write about our communications and Dr John's you know already that you have our full support. The contents of this book we leave entirely up to you. It is, so to speak, your responsibility.

Anne wondered if I should not ask you and Dr John if you had particular contents or lessons or lectures that should come into the book. What do you think about this idea?

> Bob, my friend, we feel that you are well able to choose from the communications you receive what should go into this book. Our communication is an ongoing process and therefore the book can only be a selection or excerpt of an ongoing process and cooperation. If we do have specific content which we would like you to include then we shall let you know of this in our communications.
>
> Yes, my friend, it is good that your friend Anne is supportive of this venture and that she has confidence in you to do it. Have such confidence in yourself, my friend, and the book will do well. It will reach those who have ears to hear.

Are you happy, Joshua, that we will continue for a time longer on our theme of life in Spirit?

> Bob, my friend, I am more than happy to continue with this theme. There is indeed so much to relate about how we live here in the higher spheres of life, I can hardly begin to tell you about all that we experience and do in our daily existence, though the 'daily' is not the same as it is for you on the earth plane. There is such a weaving of life, such a multiplicity of life forms and beings that it would stagger your imagination, my friend. And yet with all this multiplicity there is order and harmony. We work towards a common goal: we are united in our efforts to serve God and the good of the world. We are devoted to serving the Spirit of God in all the works that we do. This is indeed a task that fills our days with purpose and meaning. Yes there is much to do, but it is done with great joy and thankfulness.
>
> So, Bob, write your book, let it spread afar, and let those who are ready for it read it and learn from it, because you have the ability both to write and to communicate with us.

Joshua, I am still puzzled as to why I should have an ability – a telepathic ability – which it seems most or many people do not have, to communicate with those in Spirit. Why me?

> Bob, my friend, as I have explained to you many times, your particular constitution allows you this form of communication. Yes, you are right that not many possess this ability at present. But this is even more reason, my friend, why you should share and communicate what you can. In this way, others may awaken to this aptitude and be able to strike up their own communication with friends on this side of life.
>
> We wish you well, Bob, in your endeavours.

Life in Spirit

Always with you in Spirit, your friend and teacher, Joshua Isaiah.

On 30 March 2006 I wished to contact my mother in Spirit to gain reassurance for my niece's young son that he would be able to remain in communication with his own mother and father when and after he had made the great transition. (He suffers from a serious cancer condition, now medically untreatable.) This day also happened to be my fifty-ninth birthday. I received an answer from my mother about this matter.

30 March 2006

Joshua, I have just received what I believe to be a communication from my mother in answer to a question and request. Am I correct in my belief?

> Shalom, my friend. Yes indeed I can confirm that your mother was just speaking with you. She received your thoughts and responded at once with the answer to your question. This, my friend, is how love works to connect us in Spirit and in truth. You know that what you receive comes from a source other than yourself. You receive it clearly and are able to write down what you receive in your thoughts. Yes, shall we rather say in your conscious mind?
>
> So, my friend, rest assured you receive aright and can safely pass on these messages to those in need. In this you perform a worthy and needed service to others.

Later on the same day, again with Joshua, I asked: I've just watched a programme about death and dying. This makes me feel very much that a book letting people know that life continues and that communication can also continue could be very important, valuable, comforting, and true to reality. What do you think, Joshua?

> Shalom, my friend. Yes, of course, you are quite right. It is very important that people are made aware that life continues and that communication with loved ones can take place. Indeed so many on this side of life are 'dying' – longing – to speak to their loved ones, to tell them they are all right and cared for but, all too often, there is no one to hear, no one to receive their messages of love and hope and reassurance. So yes, my friend, your idea of a book is important, there is no doubt of that. I will help you as much as I can to achieve your goal. If we work together then it can be successful and bring help/comfort to many estranged souls.
> Shalom, shalom, shalom. Yours, Joshua.

No doubt my readers will themselves have many more questions to ask about the nature of life in Spirit! I know that when my niece's eleven-year-old son Mathew passed over into Spirit recently (since writing the draft of this book), his mother and father had many such very practical questions which they put to me. Of all these though, the most urgent and pressing was: 'Is he happy where he is?' The answer I received from Mathew confirmed that indeed he was.

Family Contacts and Requests

Strange as it may seem, although I have had an active interest and openness for spiritual perspectives since my youth I have, up to about nine months ago, assiduously avoided any attempts to make direct contact with those on the other side, i.e. those who have died on earth. Exactly why this has been the case, I'm not entirely sure. Certainly it had something to do with my own feeling of inferiority and unworthiness to engage in such attempts at communication. Yes, I was happy to sit with friends and read suitable contents for 'those who had died' as recommended by Rudolf Steiner in his writings and lectures. This seemed safe enough, and also of value for those who had passed over. But direct contact? No, this was not for me.

Therefore, when, through my readings from Anne, it became clear that I had the ability to do without her services for my contact with Joshua and Dr John, this came as something of a shock and surprise or, you might say, an awakening call. I therefore grasped the nettle so to speak, and gave it a try. You will understand from all that you have read so far how, again and again, I questioned whether I was on the right track – whether these were true communications, or instead fragments of my own mind, of wishful thinking, fantasy and the like. I have taken a long time to be convinced of the authenticity of the messages from or rather 'communications with' Dr John and Joshua. I have had to learn to distinguish clearly between my own thoughts and the thoughts which I am receiving from others. Thank God I don't hear voices; this would be more than I could cope with! No, it is a telepathic communication on, I think, quite a high level. No strong emotions, no sentiments, but clear unadulterated thoughts.

It was a further step for me in learning and trusting to actually turn to, and invite, contact with my parents – especially with my mother, with whom I had had very close daily physical contact for some six years or so after the death of my father. What a relief it must have been for her at the end to be released from her sick and bent body. And yet I was not there with her at the moment of death. This I regretted and felt that somehow I had failed her. I received some comfort and reassurance from Patrick Gamble, the psychic artist, when I went to see him for a private sitting on 8 May 2004. In the course of the sitting it seemed that my mother was coming through (though I, as normal, was very slow in picking up the clues she was giving me through Patrick), and at one point reference was made to 'something where you felt you could have done more, but, you could not have done more, that's the point'.

Earlier in the reading, Patrick had said that he was picking up on an 'overwhelming feeling of love' and 'a lady in Spirit connected to you'. Patrick also spoke of 'an opportunity that awaits you … a hurdle within … something that prevents the flow'. Well, looking back on these somewhat 'fragmented' communications that Patrick so kindly received for me at that sitting, and seeing these in the light of what has taken place since, I feel I understand better what was meant. I myself put obstacles – stones – in my path, and this was largely due to a lack of faith and trust in myself – at least my better self!

In the readings I requested from Anne, I sometimes asked if my parents had anything they wished to say to me. Personal though all these things are, I am prepared to share some of these communications with you the reader now, and also something of what I have received directly, telepathically. I do this once again purely out of the motive that you may be helped, supported, encouraged, by this sharing in your own efforts to make contact and to link with loved ones on the other side of life. Please take what follows in this spirit. I think my mother and father would approve of this. Remember, those that have died are 'but a thought away'.

From the first reading, sent 6 January 2005

I feel a motherly type energy coming forward and embracing you. She is shorter than you and she does not show herself, but I feel the all-pervading love she wraps round you. She is very proud of who you are and what you have become; she says, 'Who would have thought that such a scraggy lad could grow up to have the presence that you have?'

From Anne's second reading, 10 February 2005

I am given the impression of an elderly lady in Spirit a generation above you, not very tall and she tells me you were always asking questions as a child. You always had an inquisitive mind and I get the feeling you may have been a loner as a child. I am now being shown the night sky and stars; it gives me the feeling you had an interest in astronomy as a child. I am now shown a fishing rod and the feeling that comes with it is that the fishing was more important than the actual catch of the fish. This I feel is a memory...

I am now being given the impression of a gentleman in Spirit; he gives me a pain in the chest. I will ask him to clarify if it was a heart or breathing problem. He does not make it clear, but the question still remains: was it the heart or chest? This was what was in the person's mind; they were not sure to begin with, but it was the heart that gave out at the end. He is also a generation above you, I feel it is your father but he is not confirming that...

When I ask them if there is any information they would like to pass on they send their love and say life is too short for worry and to enjoy every day to the best of your abilities. Do not worry about the future because it arrives whether you worry about it or not. Your life can be more fulfilled if you concentrate on the now...

Your parents are giving me a contented feeling that they know you accept they are well in Spirit and leading their own lives. They will eventually, when it is your time, be there to meet you when you go over to Spirit. I get the feeling they may not make their presence known to you very often and this is because they feel there is not a need to do so. They are only a thought away, and I feel you often talk to them in your thoughts and they say they respond with thoughts to you and they say how lucky they are to be able to maintain that link.

I could well relate to the contents of this reading from Anne. Yes I was something of a loner, yes I had many questions, yes my hobby for some years was astronomy and yes I once caught a fish – a goldfish in the fishpond at our family home – and that was the one and only use of my new fishing rod! I felt very sorry for the fish.

From the fourth reading, 15 April 2005

As I sit to start your reading two people appear, a lady and a gentleman. The gentleman has his arm round the lady. She is dressed in a bright blue dress and they are a little hesitant in coming forward. The feeling is that it is your parents who are coming in response to your request to pass on your love to them. They have come to let you know they are with you often, including on your birthday...

> They are proud of the work you do and wish they could make their presence felt a little more. If you sit in the silence this will happen and you will feel a loving presence as they draw close to you.

From these, as it were, 'second-hand' messages I will now share something of my 'direct line', mainly with my mother, as recorded in my notebooks. The first such entry was dated 25 December 2005.

> My son, I am so glad that you wish to make contact with me this evening – this Christmas night. Your father and I are well as we live now in the spheres of Spirit. You cannot imagine, Robert, how different our life is on this side of life – this life of Spirit. We do not have to suffer the pains of earth-life through living in a body of matter. The density and darkness of matter weighs heavily on your shoulders, my son, just as it did on mine when I lived on earth. Now we are freed from all that – all that which hampered and hindered us but which also gave us the opportunity for growth and development. Yes, my son, even your father's illness was for him, and me also, a learning experience of great value. We learn through hardships and suffering, my son. This is something that you know. Take heart, Robert – you are able to do much more than you think or imagine. You yourself put limits to your abilities. You limit yourself, Robert. Have trust, my son, in yourself; have trust in your healing powers, have trust in those who want to guide and help you. Even now they stand around you more than willing to help you make the next step in your development. You must learn to trust, my son, then all will be well. You know, Robert, that this is the lesson for your present life. No other lesson is more important for you than this. You always were insecure and nervous as a child. You were frightened of your own shadow. You lacked confi-

dence in yourself. We do not judge or condemn you for this, my son. It was simply a part of life. Life is learning and learning never stops. Nor for us now in Spirit.

Robert we ask you to come to peace – to let your heart be filled with God's grace. Yes you are right, we were all worriers: too anxious and afraid of what might happen! But remember, my son, that you have the potential for change. It is something you expected of us, not so? So expect it of yourself also. But do not try too hard. Let it flow; let it come about without forcing. You always were a thinker, Robert. You always lived strongly in your thoughts; you always questioned. But now, my son, learn to trust in the spirit that guides you. Yes, even your own higher self: your own spirit. This spirit is your own best guide. Make that link to your spirit, Robert, then all will be well with you.

We are proud of what you do, of your healing work especially. We know you can do more with this. But all depends on your link with Spirit. This is where true healing comes from, my son. Robert, we will be with you – are always with you – we wait to help you just as we did in life. Call upon us when you need to. Call upon us for the help you need and we will do all that we can to assist you. Peace be with you, my son. All love from your father and me. We will always remain close and watch over you, but don't worry, we will not impose on you. You are always free to make your own decisions. You do this anyway!

All blessings, Robert, on you and your dear family. Take care of Silke; she is a precious person, whom you may rely upon. We send you our Christmas greetings and love. Yours ever, Mother and Father.

Whilst this message is clearly of a personal nature, nonetheless we see in it, as well as in all the many other communications contained in this book, how those who have died can indeed become the guides, helpers, and counsellors of those on earth. This then becomes a true cooperation between the 'living' and the so-called 'dead'; a working together for the benefit of all. There is no imposition, no coercion, no treading on the other person's toes, so to speak, but a relationship grounded in love and freedom. And this, I feel, is a healthy and strengthening relationship!

Three months passed before I sought to link up again with my parents, on the date of my mother's earthly birthday. Mother came through to speak.

11 March 2006

My dear son, thank you for contacting me on my earthly birthday. So good that you remembered, Robert. Yes, on earth I was the one who remembered all the birthdays. But that you now remember mine is a blessing indeed.

Thank you, my son. Your father and I are well here in Spirit. We live a full and joyful life. You cannot imagine, Robert, how different life is here to that which you know. It is so light and carefree that to us your life on earth seems very dark and glum.

However, there is, of course, light in the darkness. The light of Spirit can penetrate through the veil of darkness and bring light to souls who are open for it. May it come to pass, my dear, that many more, like you, are open to receive the word of the Spirit. It is not for want of trying on our part, I can assure you, that so many still remain in darkness. They do not open themselves to receive that which is close to hand, to receive that which those in Spirit wish to freely give. Yes, my dear, you are a light-bearer whether or not you realise it. You can help to shed light for others to see by. I know, Robert, that you find this difficult to accept. It is so hard to see what is in front of our noses, isn't it? But it is so that you are shedding light by what you think and do. I am proud of you for this and so is your father. He is here beside me now and he is anxious to speak to you himself. Do let him speak through you, my dear; it would give him so much pleasure.

Robert, I am here. Thank you for being open to your mother and me. We have settled into our new home and feel very content. Yes, on earth we sinned, as we all do. But God is good and makes allowances for our misdeeds and mistakes. Yes, my son, we were very close on earth and still are in Spirit. Even though you mainly have contact with Joan, I am very much present also. It was because you forged such a close bond with your mother, when I died first, that you communicate so readily with her. But do not imagine that we are not close. We will remain so in the times to come. We are closely bound – united – through destiny and karma.

I learnt so much from you, Robert, in my last life. You brought me to anthroposophy and to a new understanding of the Spirit. For this I am forever grateful. Yes, we said that we would keep in touch after I passed over and we have done so through your mother.

Yes, my illness was hard, not being able to speak, but here all is different. Here I can speak again, though not with an earthly voice. Here we communicate through thoughts, just as we are doing now. You pick up my thoughts and write them down. Yes, it is difficult to keep up with these thoughts by hand as they come through quickly and fast. But this is the wonder of the communication we can have. So Robert, my son and friend, I thank you once again for allowing me to speak to you. Your mother wants to have the final word. Yes, you see our roles are rather reversed than they were in life! God bless and take care, Robert. Your loving father.

Robert, I am here again. So good that your father spoke with you this evening on my special day. Do you remember those birthday parties in the bungalow? Yes, many old friends came and we had a happy time. Thank you for organising these happy days, Robert. We miss you and yet you are not far away and we watch with interest and love all that you do on earth, especially, of course, your healing work. So good that this continues. You will be able to help many people, Robert, and for this we are very grateful. My son, we will now withdraw because we see that your teacher in Spirit is drawing near and also wishes to speak with you this evening. God bless and keep you. Mother.

I communicated with my mother again on 26 March 2006, Mothering Sunday. The reason for this was concern over my niece's young son Mathew suffering from cancer. I include this communication here because it may bring comfort to other people who have young children who are very ill, or, for some other reason, possibly close to making the transition to the world of Spirit.

Robert, my son, thank you for wishing to speak with me today. Yes I know of your deep concerns about Mathew. Rest assured, my dear, that many are trying to help him at this time. Mathew is no longer afraid to die, this is true, but while there is life there is hope and Mathew still has plenty of life left in him.

I know, Robert, that you want to ask me if Mathew will pull through, will survive this illness. My son, I cannot tell you this. I can only tell you that whenever he makes his great transition all will be prepared for him and he will be welcomed here with open arms.

We will take care of him, rest assured.

You know, Robert, that we live now in the realms of light. Life abounds here and there is no pain and suffering such as you experience on earth. We are supported and helped in every way by beings of light. Yes, the angels, no less. So, my son, I cannot give you an answer to your question as to whether Mathew will live or die. I can only tell you that life goes on, death is an illusion, and that he will be taken care of whenever his time comes.

I would be grateful, Robert, if you will convey my words to Mathew's mother and his family. They should know that all will be well, whatever happens. Mathew is a very precious child, a special soul. We see him in his struggles on earth and yet we also see his true spirit being. A being of light and radiance. His soul shines forth for all to see, and we will not forsake him when his time comes. Tell them, Robert, of this, it will bring much comfort.

Now, my son, I think I have told you all that I can for now. What will be, will be. All of us must make the transition sooner or later. It is a loss to those on earth but it is a blessing for us in heaven to receive souls who are ready for the life here. Mathew is no longer afraid to die, and death is but the gateway to a higher and fuller life in Spirit. Our blessings and love to you Robert, to Mathew and his family.

Take care, my son. All love and blessings. Mother.

In a later communication with my mother, again concerned with Mathew's illness and his own questions, the following was included:

Always when young children pass over special conditions apply to bring as much comfort and reassurance to everyone concerned as possible.

As well as contact with members of my own family, I have, on just a few occasions so far, conveyed requests or questions on behalf of others to their loved ones in Spirit. To do this has required me to take another step in my own development of trust and clear intentionality. Clearly this involves a considerable responsibility and cannot, I feel, be done lightly. But if an earnest request comes in this way, there is also a responsibility to respond to it if at all possible. These are early days but, as with any gift a person has in life, it is there to be used, to be developed further if possible, and to be of some service to others.

Review and Looking Forward

I do not see myself as a psychic, a clairvoyant, not even as a medium. Not that I have anything against such practitioners, I hasten to add, provided, of course, their motives are pure and their abilities proven over time by their good fruits for others. Indeed, without Anne's help as a spiritual medium I would not have awoken to my own telepathic gift.

My path of development over the past seven years has been mainly in the practice of spiritual healing, to which I feel a certain vocation. However, as a spiritual healer I see myself simply as a channel, that is, a conscious and willing channel for healing energies directed by Spirit to work through me. In this sense, yes, I am therefore a medium or mediator. That I have also a certain ability to receive and send telepathic communications with those in Spirit, particularly Dr John and Joshua Isaiah so far, has come as something of an unexpected revelation, to say the least. But by now I do accept this as being the case, in spite of my repeated questionings and doubts.

Why, in fact, should it be so difficult for many of us to accept that communication and conversation, which is after all the very essence and staff of human life, should not be possible between those 'in the body' and those in Spirit? The truth is, I believe, that it is not only possible but very much wanted and needed so that we can continue our warm human fellowship. Put simply, we need each other both here and hereafter.

Looking back over the past fifteen months or so since I first struck up correspondence with Anne, the spiritual medium, and within that same period the nine months or so that I have been communicating directly with Dr John, Joshua, and more recently others, my journey has been pretty remarkable and rather rapid. It has, of course, only been possible because my potential for communication was recognised by those friends and guides on the other side. It is like so much in life – everything depends on timing. There is a right, an optimal, time for everything. If things are rushed, or premature, or somehow forced, particularly in the sphere of inner soul development, then they can go wrong and even be harmful. Slow and steady does it – coupled with patience and perseverance in learning some new ability, or unfolding a latent gift – is by far the best and safest way forward.

Often it is others, rather than ourselves, who recognise in us the abilities and gifts we already have or are able to develop. This happened to me with healing through the experienced perception and inspiration of Doreen and Dennis Fare. This has happened to me with communication through the perception of Dr John and Joshua. I can only feel extremely grateful at their faith and confidence in me when I lacked both in myself.

However, it is above all trust in oneself and in the Spirit, and in the wise guidance that works into one's life that has posed for me the biggest challenge and test. This comes through very clearly, emphatically I would say, in very many of the communications. Trust, trust, trust! This is not a matter of being asked to trust in a foolish or gullible way, it is rather to realise that trust in itself is a power – a power which opens doors. 'Ask and you will receive, knock and the door will be opened.' How often we forget to ask or to knock; not true?

Yes I am a thinker; I always have many questions. If you do not think, you also don't question things. I believe that questioning is an important activity of the human soul, of the awake individual. However, there is a difference between purely intellectual questioning and a living, over time, with important existential questions to which there are not usually, if at all, quick and simple answers.

Living now in an age of information technology, we are used to getting lots of information at the click of a mouse! But information is, I think, not the same as gaining real knowledge or wisdom. And the bottom line is that real knowledge involves gaining self-knowledge, and this is neither quick nor easy. It often comes with growing older and by learning the hard way – by the experiences of life itself. Indeed, through the very experiences and circumstances that we ourselves call forth in order to learn and grow, according to our hidden plan of life. Therefore, to understand where one is at any given point of time in one's life, it is very helpful – indispensable in fact – to do a self review. To remember and bring to mind the journey, the path, that one has been walking along. To this very much belongs recalling to mind the people that we have met and who have been there to help, guide, advise, or even challenge us at critical stages or points in our journey. Without meeting him or her just then, we say, I wouldn't have done what I did; that person really had a formative, or incisive, influence on my future path.

In this way we perceive that there is really a web of significant relationships built into our destiny and karma and this, once realised, leads to a feeling of deep gratitude and thankfulness. Our lives, we are led to recognise, are not arbitrary and left to chance and the whims of fate, but rather are wisely guided and supported. Yes, we are free to choose, to make choices, but the real inner freedom is, I believe, that we learn to acknowledge and recognise the plan, our own plan, which we have set before ourselves before we descended from Spirit into earthly life. This plan contains wisdom that is not limited to one lifetime only, but which takes account of numerous lifetimes.

We have lived in different historical periods and cultures, have had a multitude of personalities and been related to other people in all manner of different ways. The brief indications I received from Joshua in answer to my questions about my previous incarnations and my relationship to him gives much to ponder upon and consider. Such considerations can help to illuminate some of the enigmas and perplexities of one's current earth-life.

Although on the one hand I still feel astonished at where I have come to today at the time of writing this book, on the other hand, in review, many things seem to fall quite naturally into place. My questions as a child and youth about the meaning of life and death and my longing to understand what really stands behind the material world; the search for my own destiny and the clarification of my goals and aims in life; the coming, at the age of eighteen, to my first conscious awareness of spirit-knowledge through the written works of Rudolf Steiner; and, above all, the particular people that I have met and befriended along life's way.

In all this, there is a red thread to be found. It is the thread that can lead one back towards the Spirit, from whence one came, and forward towards the way ahead that remains to be revealed and lived. And what challenges, what opportunities, what possibilities lie ahead, for any and all of us, are surely exciting and enthusing. Remember, though we grow older and our physical prowess and functioning will be diminished, our spiritual and soul growth can, and in fact should, continue to advance and become more empowering and vital. Learning never stops, not in this world or the next, and with learning we gain greater knowledge, understanding, and wisdom. But however wise we may become, however enlightened our souls may be, there is one power which surpasses all else, and that is the power of love. Love is the power that unites human souls in whatever dimension of life they happen to find themselves. Bonds of love are not broken, and if we act out of love and overcome our egotism and self-centredness, then we shall know the truth and the truth will indeed set us free. The content and the tone of the communications I have received and which I have thought right to share with you in this book point clearly, I believe, to these realities. The realities that love, light, and truth can unite souls on both sides of the river; on the side of the world of the senses and matter, and on the side of the Spirit. It is love that builds, and is, the bridge that unites both.

In the well-known words of St Paul to the Corinthians, we are helped to understand what unconditional love is:

> Love is patient; love is kind and envies no one. Love is never boastful, nor conceited, nor rude; never selfish, not quick to take offence. Love keeps no score of wrongs; does not gloat over other men's sins, but delights in the truth. There is nothing love cannot face; there is no limit to its faith, its hope, and its endurance.

May I suggest that these words, taken to heart, will encourage all of us to be of service to others and to create a better, more loving and light-filled world. Our friends and guides in Spirit will no doubt help us to do this, if we ask them to.

As Joshua was at pains to point out, repeatedly, in some of his important teachings, the time has indeed come for human beings to wake up to the reality of the Spirit, and not to carry on dreaming life away in the illusion of the physical sense world. To come truly to ourselves, to recognise our own eternal light-filled spirit nature, we need to be thoroughly shaken out of the darkness of materialism and of scientific reductionism. Man is, I am convinced, neither a machine nor an animal, but an evolving spiritual being whose task it is to help transform this suffering, unique and beautiful planet into a place of love and healing. To do this we will surely need all the help we can receive from our many companions in Spirit who are but a thought away!

Conclusion

In the introduction I posed the question as to whether it really is possible to communicate with our friends and loved ones once they are no longer with us physically on earth? Is there a way, or ways, in which this is possible?

On the basis of all the communications I have received mentally, telepathically, as evidenced in this book, I have come to the unequivocal conclusion that, yes, such contact and intercourse is indeed possible between the worlds, astonishing though it may seem.

The reader will know about and probably sympathise with my own admitted doubts, questions and scepticism. These are not so much to do with any belief or knowledge gleaned from years of study and searching, and of reading the first-hand accounts of others in regard to a post-mortem Spirit existence, but much rather about my own capacities to have any direct contact with friends in Spirit. I happen to believe that scepticism, questioning, and open-mindedness are essential ingredients for a healthy and balanced view on life, and for coming to well-considered opinions and judgements. Even after having received many communications from Dr John and Joshua, I still wanted further confirmation that what I was receiving really stemmed from an independent source 'outside' me. To this end, I sent Anne a copy of one of the lengthy communications I had received from Joshua with the request that she 'check it out', so to speak: to ask Joshua if it really did come from him. I would now like to conclude this book with Joshua's words, as given to me by Anne in her ninth and last reading, dated 20 March 2006. Anne wrote:

I sat this morning and asked Joshua for his input on what you had asked in your letter. Here are his words when you ask if it was him who spoke to you:

'He knows I did. When we communicate, the 'atmosphere', the 'presence' is different than when constructing one's own thoughts. He knows truly, inwardly, that it is I communicating, but he clearly does not want his own presence to be the dominant one. I have to use his brain, his electrons, his emotions, to give empathy and understanding (and) that is why it is complex to define who is who. We blend together to become more than two individuals.

'He allows me access to his most inner being; if he did not truly accept it was me he would not allow the process. Give him my everlasting and enduring love as you, his friend, pass on my thoughts by putting vibrations on paper – the truth that I do exist – because by questioning himself by default he questions me. I truly am Spirit and I will serve the divine to the best of my humble ability and if I find Bob's mind interfering in our communications I will withdraw and explain to him then or later, depending on the circumstances, what had occurred and how to avoid it in the future. This is said to reassure him as I have every faith in him as my communicator to the physical. Shalom. Joshua.

Anne concluded her reading by saying:

Keep up the work, Bob; he truly is a lovely man, keep in contact.
In love, light and truth always. Anne.

Suggested Reading

Hopefully the books listed here are still in print and available. I have read them, or part of them at least, over the years but have deliberately not turned to them myself during the time of receiving communications from Spirit, in order not to be influenced by their fascinating contents.

Bamford, C [ed.], *Staying Connected*, Anthroposophic Press, 1999

Bittleston, A, *Our Spiritual Companions*, Floris Books, 1980

Deverell, D, *Light beyond the Darkness*, Temple Lodge, 1996

Greaves, H, *Testimony of Light*, The World Fellowship Press Ltd, 1969

Reisch, G, *A Book of the Dead*, Gerhard Reisch Publishing, 2005

Steiner, R, *Angels – Selected Lectures*, London, Rudolf Steiner Press, 1996

Wetzl, J, *The Bridge over the River*, The Anthroposophic Press, 1974

White, R and Swainson, M, *Gildas Communicates*, Neville Spearman, 1971

White Eagle, *Heal Thyself*, Hampshire, The White Eagle Publishing Trust, 1987

Woodward, B, *Spirit Healing*, Floris Books, 2004

In addition, there are, of course, the many popular books by Betty Shine and Doris Stokes, both of whom were well-known and respected mediums.

From the anthroposophical perspective, there are books containing lecture courses specifically on the theme of life between death and rebirth, given by Rudolf Steiner in the first quarter of the twentieth century, as well as single lectures by him on this subject, available from Rudolf Steiner Press, London, or Anthroposophic Press, New York.

The White Eagle Publishing Trust publishes and distributes the wise teachings of White Eagle in numerous interesting books.

Anne Lewis, the spiritual medium, is happy to be contacted by email: annelewis@postmaster.co.uk.

Postscript

This evening on 12 April 2006, the day before my manuscript goes to be typed, I asked Joshua and John two questions: may I ask if you both feel happy with the book I've written? Is there anything else you want me to include?

Joshua came through to answer these questions. I feel I should include the answers as they were given me, in full.

> Shalom, my friend. Yes I am here with you now and I am happy to answer your questions, also on behalf of John.
>
> Bob, the book you have written has gone well. Yes, my friend, it was a real deed to write such a book. Both John and I wish the book well. As I have said before, the book will bring much comfort to those who are ready to accept its contents. It may, however, also bring much criticism from those who are not ready to accept it. No matter, my friend, you have done your part. It is up to others to decide how they will take it.
>
> Well done, my friend. John and I both send you our congratulations on completing the book. Yes, it will be interesting to see who will eventually publish this work. As you say, Bob, to have the widest possible access to members of the public should be an important consideration. We shall watch with great interest to see how things develop.
>
> Now, as to your second question, Bob. Yes, there is something else John and I would still wish you to include. It is this, my friend: we feel that you should include the following words, my friend.

Love lives in the light and in the light the power of love holds sway when angel messengers unite with thoughts of men to bring the world to harmony and to peace.

This is the goal for which mankind should strive, and these are the words we would like you to include, my friend. All blessings to you.
Shalom, shalom, shalom, from myself and Dr John.

I read these words back once more and asked Joshua if I had them aright.

Yes, my friend, you have received the words aright and yes, I can confirm that we would like you to add these words in your book. All blessings, my friend, and thank you for contacting us this evening.
Shalom, my friend, and goodnight for now.

This is then now really the end of the book, not least because my pen is just about to run out of ink!
All blessings to you.

Printed in the United Kingdom
by Lightning Source UK Ltd.
119251UK00001B/1-9